"Untapped Brilliance *is brilli*
a person how to get to the
from the clutter and frustratio
hope and practical wisdom, this book is a treasure."

— EDWARD HALLOWELL, M.D.
Author of *Driven to Distraction*

"Untapped Brilliance *is a little gem of a self-coaching primer. In straightforward language Jacqueline Sinfield provides practical advice and simple, easy-to-follow techniques that will help adults challenged by ADHD to re-create their lives."*

— GABOR MATÉ, M.D.
Author of *Scattered Minds: A New Look at the Origins and Healing of Attention Deficit Disorder*

"From the outside, I appeared to "have it all" - an interesting career, a comfortable income, and a supportive husband. My inner self was quite different, however. Because I have ADHD, I frequently felt overwhelmed by my life. I thought, "OK, so I have ADHD. Now what? How can I regain control over my life? Thank heavens for Jacqueline's life-affirming book, Untapped Brilliance! Since I started following her simple but highly effective strategies for dealing with ADHD, life is not only manageable but also enjoyable. My self esteem is on the rise and I am pursuing a long-standing dream at work. ADHD is no longer the albatross it once seemed."

— L.R.
A 60-year-old physician, Montreal, QC.

"After following the suggestions outlined in Jacqueline's fabulous book, I found that many of the small steps not only lead to an obvious benefit that is measured by more production at work, but also adds to the quality and enjoyment of life, as if the blur and frenzy I used to experience has slowed down, giving me a chance to smell the profound scent that is life. Thank you, Jacqueline."

— GARY MALLALIEU
A 40-year-old teacher

"Living with unmanaged ADHD had left me deeply discouraged. A single mom of 2 small boys at 42 … I was also recovering from bankruptcy, barely able to hold a job, practically friendless and completely exhausted from the constant struggle just to keep my head above water. Then I found Jacqueline Sinfield. Following her 11-fold path finally has me flowing with the current, not caught in the eddies! Now I'm happily cultivating a nurturing, anger-free home for my children and channeling my wellspring of ideas into exciting achievements: a circle of wonderful friends, a figure drawing portfolio and a healthy bank account balance!"

— M.A.
A 42-yr-old translator, Montreal, Quebec

"Having read and followed the advice in *Untapped Brilliance* I have gone from feeling frustrated and overwhelmed by day-to-day activities to finally getting my life in order and actually achieving my goals. Buy this book! it will change your life!!"

— PETER BAILEY
Director of Recruitment Flow Consulting

"Creative, methodical and enlightening! Jacqueline's approach has proven very efficient in helping me reach both my professional and personal goals."

— YSABEL VIAU
Strategic development, marketing & communications consultant

"As a spouse of someone with ADHD, I found this book very interesting and informative. It has helped me to better understand ADHD, and how I can help my husband to reach his potential."

— G.B.
A 49-year-old manager, Montreal, Quebec

"Jacqueline Sinfield has captured the essence of how to assist adults with ADHD. In Untapped Brilliance she gives the reader simple and effective steps to achieve optimum potential in order to lead a happy and fulfilling life. It's time to untap the brilliance and shine! Bravo Jacqueline!"

— DR. LINO DIFOGLIO
Chiropractor

"A few months ago, I was feeling a little depressed. I had recently moved to a new country and was struggling to settle down. After working with Jacqueline and following some of the steps outlined in her book I have noticed a big difference. I am now feeling more emotionally stable, interact better socially, feel and look healthier (I lost 14 lbs), and no longer feel the sadness I used to feel. I am able to be productive on a daily basis, which results in me feeling in control and good about myself and my life as I move towards my life goals."

— S.S.
A 24-year-old student

"I can commend the steps described in Jacqueline's book: they have greatly improved my quality of life, beyond what words can tell… not forgetting the importance of the constructive mindset accompanying every step."

— M. L.
A 60-year-old teacher (special education)

Untapped
BRILLIANCE

HOW TO REACH
YOUR FULL POTENTIAL
AS AN ADULT
WITH ADHD

JACQUELINE SINFIELD

Untapped Brilliance: How to Reach Your Full Potential
As an Adult with ADHD

Copyright © 2008 Jacqueline Sinfield

First edition published 2008
Second edition published 2022

All rights reserved. No part of this book may be reproduced or transmitted in any form or by any means, electronic or mechanical including photography, recording or any information storage and retrieval system without written permission from the author and publisher.

ISBN: 9798354831685

Cover design, layout and typesetting by Cyanotype Book Architects

Independently Published

Important Note

This book contains information and education. It is not providing medical advice, mental health advice, therapy, or the diagnosis or treatment of a condition or illness. Please seek medical advice for any medical or mental health conditions. Your doctor, medical advisor, mental health advisor, and/or therapist should be consulted before you begin a new diet, exercise program, or other lifestyle changes.

Author's Note

In this book I have used examples from my clients who I have had the pleasure of meeting in my coaching practice. To protect their identities and to ensure the utmost in confidentiality, there have been description and identity changes. Examples of my family and myself have not been changed.

Table of Contents

Introduction		13
Step One	Mega Omega	19
Step Two	Nourish Yourself	25
Step Three	Daily Exercise	37
Step Four	Meditation 101	45
Step Five	Get a Good Night's Sleep	51
Step Six	Thrive in Your Enviornment	57
Step Seven	Set Goals That Excite You	69
Step Eight	Staying on Track	79
Step Nine	Boost Your Self-Esteem	95
Step Ten	Create a Group of Wonderful People in Your Life	109
Step Eleven	Have Fun!	121
Congratulations!		131
Appendix A: Emergency ADHD Tool Box		133
Appendix B: ADHD Primer		135
Appendix C: Charts		143
Appendix D: Recommended Resources		163

Introduction

One snowy Montreal morning, Barry, my 10:00 client, walked into my office with a big smile on his face. This was a very good sign as when he first started visiting me he had been in very low spirits. After removing his snow boots and taking off his coat, he asked:

"Guess what day it is today?"

"Hmmmm," I thought, because nothing sprung to mind. I knew it wasn't his birthday, but I tried that anyway. No, this was not his birthday.

"Guess again!" he said. Perhaps an obscure holiday that I wasn't familiar with? No, that wasn't it either. I tried a few more guesses and then Barry told me that today was "Coach Appreciation Day." It wasn't a nationally known holiday, but it was Barry's coach appreciation day.

Barry wanted to thank me enthusiastically for the dramatic improvements he had seen in his life over the six months he had been visiting me. By working together and using the 11 steps outlined in this book, Barry was starting to feel and see the difference in his body and in his life. He looked physically healthier; his skin had a healthy glow (replacing a dull gray pallor) and his eyes had a sparkle where before they had been red and tired. His pot-belly was practically non- existent and his shoulders seemed broader.

However, the physical differences were a secondary benefit; the most important changes were the ones that had happened internally. Barry reported feeling calmer and happier and had more confidence in his abilities and strengths. He had put the brakes on the craziness of his life, and now rather than reacting to everything around him, he was in control. He was having more time to enjoy his family and friends and was now taking steps to achieve his life goals.

The 'Untapped Brilliance' Story

The 11 steps that comprise this book were developed to help solve a problem I repeatedly hear from my clients, which is, "I have so much potential; why can't I seem to achieve what I know I am capable of?"

I could see for myself how amazing the people were. But it was as if they were standing in a swamp where the mud was weighing them down, making it really hard to maintain status quo, let alone move forward.

I realized there must be a way to untap the brilliance of these incredible people so they could release all their potential.

The steps in 'Untapped Brilliance' form a strong foundation which, when in place, minimizes the negative aspects of ADHD and allows all the magical and wonderful qualities of ADHD to be realized. The 11 steps that help to build this foundation fall into three categories: Physical Body, Internal Environment, and External Environment.

Physical Body
Omega 3, food, exercise, sleep

Internal Environment
Goals, meditation, self-esteem, time management

External Environment
Organized environment, good people, fun

Consequently, these three elements became the 'Brilliance System." This is a method by which adults with ADHD can untap their previously unrealized brilliance and achieve their true potential.

My Story

As a little girl, I wanted to be a nurse when I grew up because I loved helping people. I was also fascinated by people getting answers to their problems.

When I visited my Nana, I would make a beeline for her *Woman's Weekly* magazines because they had an agony aunt column. I would take the magazine stack to a quiet corner. I didn't want to be discovered by any adults in case they though it was weird for a 12-year-old to be reading about menopause and marriage problems.

My career path had some logical steps. I qualified and worked as a Registered Nurse in England. I got an Honors degree in psychology.

There were also some 'lucky' moments that I couldn't have planned. For example, one day, when I was at a career crossroads, I happened to see Oprah interviewing a Life Coach. It was the first time I had ever heard of a Life Coach, and I had a light bulb moment: "That's it! I'll be a Coach!"

When I graduated from a three-year coaching program, the general public still didn't know about coaches, but adults with ADHD did. I would get calls from ADHDers asking if I could help them. I could! All the information I learned from my formal education, combined with the techniques I used to help myself, as someone with severe dyslexia, helped my clients to see amazing results. Now, every week I am jokingly asked things like,

"Are you psychic?"

"Do you have my house bugged?"

Just yesterday, a member of The Untapped Brilliance Facebook group wrote: "Every. Single. Day: you get inside my head. You really know this condition inside and out, and you're doing a great job as an educator and advocate."

Although ADHD and dyslexia are different conditions, having dyslexia allows me to really understand ADHD. Like my ADHD clients and readers, I know what it's like to live for years with an undiagnosed condition and to live in a world that wasn't designed for how my brain works. I also know what helps!

In this book, you will learn the 11 steps in my system. This system has been the foundation of my ADHD coaching for nearly two decades. It brings extraordinary success to my 1:1 clients and to my Untapped Brilliance Club membership clients.

It will help you, too!

How to Use This Book

Read the book with an open mind. You may have heard some of the information before, or feel that some of the steps are very easy and so you might believe that you are doing them even if you have just read them. But it is important to both read the information and implement the steps into your life. It is by taking action that you will feel and experience the results and benefits.

You don't have to read this book cover to cover, although you might want to skim through it all, so you have an overview. Instead, think of this book as your friendly guide keeping you company as you go on this exciting personal journey.

At the back of the book are charts to help you with the exercises in the book. If you'd like to download a printable version, go to **www.untappedbrilliance.com/chartsfromthebook**

For bonus points, get a binder and make your very own Untapped Brilliance Binder! It's a great way to feel organized and record your progress. Your binder also acts as a visual reminder of all the new things you are incorporating into your life.

Another way to keep your motivation up and interest piqued is to go to the Untapped Brilliance website blog:

www.untappedbrilliance.com/blog. It's a treasure trove of articles that will supplement the topics you are about to read.

OK! We are all set for a fun and rewarding journey together to help your Untapped Brilliance shine brighter than ever before. Sit down, put your feet up, and turn the page to Step One!

STEP ONE

Mega Omega

"Omega 3 fatty acids.... every cell in your body needs them"
— **Dr. Cathleen London**

Why Are Omega 3 Fatty Acids So Important for People With ADHD?

Since ADHD is neurological in nature, it is very important that your brain receives all the nutrients it requires to function at its peak. Omega 3 is one of the most important nutrients for optimum brain function because it increases the levels of neurotransmitters.

Omega 3 is one of the essential fatty acids. They are termed 'essential' because they are essential for life. 'Fatty acids' are the necessary structural blocks that make up fats and oils. While we have been told that fats are bad, this is not totally true. We do need good fat in our diet, and essential fatty acids are the 'good' fats.

There are two principal groups of essential fatty acids: Omega 3 and Omega 6. While these two fatty acids are crucial to good health, the body can't manufacture them, so they must come from your diet. Omega 6 is already plentiful in our regular diets, so we don't need to worry about getting enough. However, Omega 3 is much less readily available, so we need to make a conscious effort to ensure that we consume enough.

Neurons in the brain release neurotransmitters. There are many neurotransmitters. Here are a few of the more well known ones: dopamine, endorphins, norepinephrine, and acetylcholine. Dopamine is responsible for action, and when dopamine levels are reduced, your attention span is also reduced. Omega 3 essential fatty acids enhance the amount of dopamine in the brain, which is the same job that prescription ADHD medications do. While at the moment there is no exact research to support this, we can infer that dietary Omega 3 is important for anyone with ADHD.

The benefits of Omega 3 you are most likely to notice within the first month are: increased ability to concentrate, increased calmness and improved memory.

Taking an Omega 3 supplement is an important and easy step toward achieving your full potential. This is my first recommendation because it's the easiest to carry out, and the benefits can be huge. And higher levels of Omega 3 will actually make the other steps much easier for you!

What Depletes Neurotransmitters?

While Omega 3 increases neurotransmitters, other factors deplete them, such as:

Age
It is thought that as many as 60 percent of adults over age 40 have neurotransmitter deficiencies. This is because older cells generate smaller amounts of neurotransmitters, and cell receptors are less responsive to them.

Extended Periods of Emotional or Physical Stress
Neurotransmitters help the body cope with stressful experiences. As stress continues they become depleted.

Medications
Long term use of antidepressants and stimulants can drain neurotransmitters.

Neurotoxins
High levels of caffeine, alcohol, nicotine, ingested metals, recreational drugs and chemical pesticides are toxic to your brain. They harm the neurons and reduce neurotransmitter production.

Poor Eating Habits/Low Calorie Diets
Nutrients in food are the building blocks for neurotransmitter production, so any diet that reduces the levels of available nutrients can adversely affect neurotransmitter levels.

Unusual Sleep Patterns
Lack of sleep or insomnia also depletes neurotransmitters.

How Much Omega 3 Should I Take?

Speak to your doctor about the best dose of Omega 3 for you because even though Omega 3 has many helpful benefits, there can be side effects, too. Possible side effects range from an upset stomach to changing how your body uses prescribed medication, including any ADHD medication you take. Omega 3 can also act as a blood thinner. So, although Omega 3 is readily available in stores, it's still good to treat it with respect.

What Foods Are Rich in Omega 3?

Types of Fish That Contain the Most Omega 3
Salmon (1,000 times the Omega 3 of cod)
Wild salmon (has the perfect ratio of Omega 3 to Omega 6)
Herring
Mackerel
Rainbow trout
Sardines
Tuna

Other Foods
Flaxseed
Walnuts
Certain vegetable oils (i.e., canola oil, flaxseed oil, and walnut oil)
Dark green leafy vegetables (i.e., spinach and kale)

Where Can You Buy Omega 3 Supplements?

Omega 3 is available from a wide variety of sources. Most likely your local health food store will have a good stock of Omega 3, as will your pharmacy. The internet is also a a great place to locate Omega 3, as will your pharmacy. Dr. Barry Sears (who created The Zone diet and does research on Omega 3 and health) sells pharmeceutical-grade fish oil on his website, **www.drsears.com**, both in liquid and capsule form. If you don't like swallowing tablets, the liquid is a great option! This product is more expensive but it's worth the investment. Vegetarian versions of Omega 3 are also available, although they may be a bit harder to find.

Don't stress out about finding the "perfect" Omega 3. It's much better to just start with what you can easily get.

ACTIONS

1. Check with your doctor before taking Omega 3 supplements. Although Omega 3 is vital for brain functioning, supplements may be inadvisable for some health conditions and could interact adversely with certain medications.

2. Buy an Omega 3 supplement.

3. Start adding foods rich in Omega 3 to your diet. (We will be talking more about food in the next chapter.)

4. Notice and enjoy the benefits!

5. There is a lot more to say about ADHD and Omega 3! If you'd like to learn more, head to this article on the Untapped Brilliance blog:
   www.untappedbrilliance.com/omega

STEP TWO

Nourish Yourself

"Let your food be your medicine, and your medicine be your food."
— **Hippocrates**

Why Is Food So Important If You Have ADHD?

The food we eat is as powerful as any drug you could be prescribed. It affects our body, both short- and long-term. The long-term effects of poor eating are very well documented, and include strokes and heart disease. The short-term effects of food might be lesser known and yet are critical for a person with ADHD as there is a direct link between the food you consume and how effectively the brain can operate. A healthy diet can help to minimize the negative effects of ADHD. Even if you are one of those people who 'eat to live' (rather than 'live to eat'), it is really important to take care of what you eat. If it helps, make a mental switch and think that you are feeding your brain, not just your body.

Due to the changes in our diet in the last century, we've gone from eating pure, whole foods to processed foods, and we now need to become conscious of consuming essential fatty acids.

For the ADHD person, eating is not always the easiest thing. Preparing food takes time, focus and planning ahead. Also, if you are on medication, it can take your appetite away and food can lose its appeal.

When clients come and see me for their first session, I ask them to tell me all the food they eat in a typical day. This gives me a clear insight into what food is helping and what is hindering them. What we usually find is a diet that is comprised of mostly simple carbohydrates, lesser quality protein, and long delays between meals.

What Foods Will Benefit You the Most?

You need plenty of high-quality protein, a healthy amount of good fat (and very little bad fat), good carbohydrates and lots of water—all consumed steadily throughout the day.

Protein

Eating protein daily is essential. It provides energy and is needed to mend muscles and body tissues, as well as produce antibodies, enzymes, hormones, and maintain the balance of acid and alkali in the system.

Eating protein from a variety of food sources each day helps to ensure your body gets the essential amino acids it needs. Amino acids are the building blocks for neurotransmitters, which as we've seen are crucial for optimal brain functioning. Research has established that lack of protein in the diet can diminish neurological functioning.

This is particularly important for people with ADHD, who find that a meal including good quality protein minimizes ADHD symptoms. Providing your brain with the nutrition it requires helps it maintain the correct chemical balance and carry out the functions you rely on it for. You'll be better able to pay attention, solve problems, concentrate, remember things and maintain a stable mood and emotions.

However, some sources of protein are high in calories, so remember that only a relatively small amount is required daily, as part of a balanced diet. Some good-quality proteins are:

- Chicken and turkey (white meat)
- Lean red meat
- Fish
- Protein powder
- Dairy products
- Legumes (kidney beans, lentils, etc.) and carbohydrates (i.e., brown rice, corn, nuts, seeds or wheat products, etc.) combine to form a complete protein for vegetarian diets

Fats

Our brain is composed of around 60 percent fat. Since brain cells are principally made up of fat, it is vital that your diet provides the *right* kind of fat for optimum brain health.

Fats are often referred to as 'good' fats (i.e., mono-saturated or polyunsaturated) and 'bad' fats (i.e., saturated or hydrogenated.) The 'bad' fats are likely to cause disease in the future and sabotage your mental well-being in the short term.

The 'bad' fats come mostly from animal products: fatty meats and dairy products. They contribute to high cholesterol and high triglyceride levels, which can result in cardiovascular disease. High consumption of these 'bad' fats could also lead to certain types of cancer.

Hydrogenated fats (or trans fats)

These fats are found in packaged foods, and are worse for our health than saturated fats. They raise the 'bad' LDL cholesterol levels and decrease the 'good' HDL cholesterol.

Monounsaturated fats
These fats are good for you since they do not raise cholesterol. They can be found in nuts and nut butters, avocados, and olive oil.

Polyunsaturated fats
These fats are divided into two major categories, Omega 3 and Omega 6 fatty acids. These fats are actually good for us, as they lower triglycerides. The body uses Omega 3 to produce substances similar to hormones with anti-inflammatory effects. They avert heart attacks and strokes and assist the body's sugar-insulin metabolism, in addition to all the other fabulous benefits mentioned in Step One.

Carbs - The Good and the Bad

The Bad Carbs
Simple carbohydrates such as white bread, white pasta and rice, processed cereals, sugary snacks, chocolate, candies, junk food, and corn are all problematic. Because they are quickly broken down and metabolized by the body, they give you a blast of energy, but also cause an excessive amount of insulin to be produced. This in turn causes tiredness, inattention, lack of focus, and scattered thinking-- the exact symptoms that people with ADHD are trying to overcome!

People who eat high-carbohydrate diets also experience large swings in their blood sugar levels. The brain requires an even and constant supply of glucose, and when blood sugar levels drop rapidly, neurons can no longer function properly. Optimal brain functioning requires that you reduce your consumption of simple carbohydrates.

Simple carbohydrates are comfort foods. They make us feel warm and contented because they release dopamine. However, there are other ways to get your dopamine flowing, such as exercise and meditation.

The Good Carbs
Complex carbs such as beans, legumes, vegetables and whole grains have all their fiber in its natural state. Therefore, your body processes them more slowly, for a more long-lasting and controlled release of energy. You don't get that quick high and plummeting low like you do with simple carbs. Your body does need some carbohydrates for energy, so select complex carbs instead of simple ones.

Eating Regularly Throughout the Day

Your brain needs a constant flow of energy from the food you consume. It doesn't want peaks and valleys caused by big meals and then long periods of no food. The benefits of eating regularly throughout the day include:

- Calmness
- Reduced anxiety
- More physical energy
- More mental energy
- "I can" attitude
- Improved mental focus
- Less fidgety
- Less brain fog
- Less emotional turbulence

What Are Some Good Snacks?
When we think about snacks, typically our mind goes to the naughty foods that we know are not good for us, but taste so good! However, in this book when I mention a snack, I am referring to a healthy snack. Sorry!

It is important to eat three meals and two or three snacks throughout the day to keep your physical and mental energy steady.

If you just eat three or, even worse, only two meals a day, your energy level will fluctuate enormously. At meal time you are eating large amounts, and your body uses lots of energy to digest this food, which is why you feel sleepy after lunch. Between meals, there are long periods when you are burning more calories than you are consuming. This makes for low energy, irritability, and a generally reduced level of mental functioning. If you eat healthy snacks you'll be less hungry at mealtimes. You will naturally eat less and avoid ups and downs between meals.

Healthy snacks might include:

- Fruit
- Cheese
- A boiled egg
- Cottage cheese with some fruit
- A handful of nuts (almonds are great)
- Yogurt
- V8 juice

Making the Transition

Changing your food habits is not always easy, because eating involves so much more than just consuming food for energy. Food is linked to social behavior and cultural rituals. It can conjure up memories of childhood or it can be used as a treat or for comfort during tough times.

So there's more to this step than just cultivating new habits and tastes. It can be helpful to shift your mindset as well! You might need to learn a bit about nutrition (this book is a great start!) along with some new cooking techniques. The good news about dietary changes is that there are no side effects, many positive effects, and the results are long lasting! Some people like to go straight into a new diet, while others like to transition slowly from their existing one. Do whatever feels right for you.

Cooking and eating healthy food is a way to nurture and take care of yourself. You might not be used to making this effort, but the payoff is worth it.

Grocery shopping and preparation may take longer at first, but once you get used to your new way of eating it will become second nature.

Diets

For some clients, following an eating plan or having other external guidelines makes the transition easier. It takes the brain work out of creating a new eating plan or deciding what to have for every meal or snack.

Below I describe three healthy eating plans that follow the basic principles of an ADHD-friendly eating style. Choose whichever one seems the most appropriate given your personality and tastes.

The Zone Diet (Dr. Barry Sears)
This approach focuses on good quality protein and lots of good carbs. Dr. Sears has written a number of Zone books, including "The Omega RX Zone" which emphasizes the benefits of eating lots of Omega 3 and describes the impact of eating 'in the zone' on many conditions, including ADHD.

Perricone Diet (Nicholas Perricone, MD)
Dr. Perricone's diet helps to reduce inflammation and is rich in Omega 3. His food plan includes three meals and two snacks and is easy to follow. There are several different books available by Dr. Perricone, all with the same helpful framework.

Noom

Noom is an app that encourages healthy eating habits. No foods are off limits. However, by using a color-coded system, you are naturally guided to eat more fresh fruits and vegetables ("green" foods) and fewer sweets and high-unhealthy-fat foods ("orange" foods.) ADHDers are visual, so color-coding is beneficial in all areas of life, including your diet.

Making Dietary Changes

It can be daunting to start a new eating plan, and too many changes at once can be overwhelming. When I run into this problem with my clients, I give them a simple piece of advice which seems to work for almost everyone: one meal at a time.

I suggest making your breakfast ADHD friendly first. When you are comfortable with breakfast, focus on your evening meal. When that's second nature, work on lunch (which is the most difficult because it is often eaten outside of the home).

The first step is to go through your cupboards and get rid of all your unhealthy products and then go on a shopping trip to replace them with healthy alternatives.

Breakfast

Breakfast is the most important meal of the day, yet many people skip it. Some people are not hungry in the morning, some don't feel they have the time, and some just can't face the hassle of making a meal first thing in the morning! One great solution is a quick and easy nutrition-packed smoothie.

If this option appeals to you, try the 'magic protein smoothie' recipe below that I recommend to all my clients. It provides the all-important protein along with a nice helping of fruit. This really kick starts your brain for the day!

Magic Protein Smoothie
- 1 cup of frozen berries
- 1 scoop of protein powder (the protein powder comes with a measuring scoop)
- Enough water to be able to blend everything smoothly
- Spoonful of nut butter
- Blend and enjoy!

This is the basic recipe, and clients have told me of many ways they have changed it to suit their tastes. You could try different berries, add a banana or handful of spinach, use milk or your favorite milk substitute instead of water ... the possibilities are endless!

Dinner
Once you have breakfast figured out, you can start thinking about how to improve your evening meal. Take the emphasis off simple carbohydrates and focus more on protein. So rather than eating a plate of pasta, have a grilled chicken breast, lots of fresh vegetables and a small portion of brown rice.

Locate your nearest health food shop. More than a place to stock up on healthy items, it may also inspire you to try new dishes at home. Healthy doesn't have to be boring and tasteless! In fact, once your taste buds adjust (and you become accustomed to feeling better mentally and physically all day long!) a trip to the health food store will have your mouth watering!

Lunch
When you are comfortable with your new breakfast and dinner choices, its time to shake up lunchtime. If you decide to brown-bag it, leftovers from the night before are a good solution, or you can pack something that travels well, like a big chicken salad. If you're having lunch out, make a healthy choice about where to eat **ahead of time**, before you get hungry and start craving a less healthy option!

Snacks

After taming breakfast, dinner and finally lunch, this part is easy: have healthy snacks on hand at home, in the car and at work.

Easy and Effortless

Try to think of ways to make preparing and cooking food for yourself as easy and effortless as possible. Consider investing in a George Foreman grill since it drains all the fat away, and is an effortless way to cook your protein and some vegetables, usually in 30 minutes or less!

Joining Costco is a good idea. It's the perfect one-stop-shop where you can buy your frozen berries, frozen veggies, salmon, grain-fed chicken, salad, almonds in bulk ... and it's all great quality food!

Keep a shopping list on your fridge so you can jot down items you run out of. Find a way to organize your new recipes so you have easy access to them.

Vitamins

There is a lot of information out there about vitamins. It is often confusing to know what and how much to take and if your diet is providing you with what you need. To help with this dilemma, I recommend that you visit the website **www.realage.com**.

This is a marvelous website created by Dr. Roizen and his team. Dr. Roizen is a cardiologist and he wanted to motivate people to take better care of their bodies. When trying to work out how to achieve this, he realized everyone wants to be youthful. Some people are younger physiologically and mentally than their calendar age since they are active and take care to make healthy eating choices. Dr. Roizen came up with an assessment and guidelines to show everyone how to reduce their calendar age.

After filling out a comprehensive questionnaire, you will be advised as to what vitamins you should take based on your age, gender, and other lifestyle factors.

Water

Our brain is made up of 85 percent water. In order to keep it working at its optimal function, we need to drink lots of water. Without enough water, our concentration becomes shorter, memory worsens and we become moody, depressed and fatigued. The brain also needs oxygen, and the more hydrated the body is, the more oxygen is available. It is thought that an adult loses 10 cups of fluid each day, even without exercising. As the body can't absorb large quantities of water at a time, drinking smaller amounts more often is the key. Drink a glass as soon as you wake up, and another before bed.

Aim for ten 8-oz. glasses a day. Be guided by your body. Your requirements will differ every day, depending on the room or outdoor temperature and your exercise level. Also, if you consume drinks such as coffee and alcohol, you will need more water to counterbalance the effects from these dehydrating beverages.

Being conscious of how much water you drink is the first step to consuming more water. Then it's a question of developing new strategies and habits to ensure you are increasing your water intake. For example, carry a bottle of water with you whenever you go out, and keep a bottle in your car to drink going to and from work and while you run errands. Consider purchasing a home water-filter system since they are inexpensive and make your water more palatable. Having a jug of water in your fridge with some lime or lemon slices in it makes the water extra tasty.

ACTIONS

1. Write down what you eat in a typical day, starting with breakfast, ending in any bedtime feasts, and all the meals, snacks and drinks in between.

2. Think of things that will motivate you. What will the personal benefits be? Write a list of both ADHD-related and non-ADHD-related benefits a change in your diet would bring you.

3. Eat three meals and two or three snacks a day.

4. Include protein in every meal and snack.

5. Visit the website **www.realage.com**

6. Learn more about breakfast and ADHD here:
   www.untappedbrilliance.com/the-adhd-breakfast

7. Think of five ways that you could increase your water intake.

8. Start to notice the difference in your mental clarity, your energy and emotions.

STEP THREE

Daily Exercise

"If you are too busy to exercise, you are too busy"
— **Edwin C. Bliss**

In today's world, we lead a sedentary life compared to previous generations. Rather than exercise being an integral part of our lives, we have to make a conscious decision to exercise. The good news is that regular exercise has many rewards for all aspects of your well-being: physically, mentally and psychologically.

Most of my ADHD clients know the benefits of exercise, not just through what the media has told them, but from their own personal observations. They know when they exercise they feel better and their ADHD symptoms lessen.

The benefits of exercise on your long-term health are well documented and include a healthy heart, reduced risk of type 2 diabetes and the maintenance of a healthy weight. We are going to focus here on the benefits of exercise on ADHD symptoms. Exercise does all of the following:

Improves attention	Lessens bouts of depression
Increases mental focus	Improves body image (and self-esteem)
Improves cognitive function (memory)	Improves your mood
Increases alertness	Reduces negative feelings
Expends pent up energy. If you are hyperactive, you will be able to sit still longer	Helps you to regain a sense of control
Clears mental cobwebs	Induces pride in oneself
Allows you to focus on the task at hand	Allows you to become more proactive, and less reactive
Boosts mental stamina	Helps you to develop a more positive outlook
Improves sleep patterns	Reduces anxiety

Aerobic vs. Non-aerobic Exercise

There are two types of exercise, aerobic and non-aerobic. Aerobic exercise provides the best type of workout for people with ADHD.

Aerobic Exercise

Aerobic exercise is when continued exertion occurs, and the lungs are worked strongly. Examples include running, biking, rowing, fast walking, and swimming. When a period of continual exertion is maintained the body's chemistry changes. The intense exercise increases blood flow in the brain as well as oxygen. Also, you'll experience increased levels of endorphins and acetylcholine which help alleviate ADHD symptoms. This helps you focus, creates greater mental alertness, and instills a sense of calm, both directly after the exercise period and in the long term.

The increase in blood flow and oxygen also encourages higher neurotransmitter production levels. However, this can only happen if your body has consumed the right type of nutrients, particularly Omega 3. To get the absolute most from your workouts, be sure to take your Omega 3.

Non-aerobic Exercise
Non-aerobic (or anaerobic) exercise is a different type of exercise because rather than continued exertion there is a 'stop and start' series of motions.

For example, weight training, housework, gardening and golf are considered non-aerobic exercise. While weight training is still important as part of a healthy lifestyle, it is the intense aerobic exercise that will benefit your ADHD brain. You might also want to speak to a trainer at your local gym to design a workout program specifically for you.

Psychological Benefits of Exercise

One of the psychological benefits of exercise is that when it becomes a habit, it is something you will feel really proud of. You will be doing something positive for yourself and it is something to take pride in. When you start working out, other things fall into place. Besides your ADHD symptoms lessening, it will be easier for you to be organized, and you will actually crave healthier foods and more water. You will look forward to exercising. After adopting an exercise routine, you will start to feel more on top of your life, more in control, clearer and more focused. Exercise gives you a sense that anything is possible. You will be someone who exercises every day!

Exercise is also good for your emotions, as it gives you a chance to mull problems over and let go of any bad feelings about certain issues you may be keeping inside of you. Also, the endorphins that your body releases when you exercise give you a good feeling.

Consult a Fitness Expert

If you are doing lots of exercise, it's important that you have health experts in your corner. You certainly don't want an injury to stop you from exercising, so find a physiotherapist, chiropractor, or osteopath you like and have their telephone numbers on hand in case of an injury. You might want to see a podiatrist as well to find out if you would benefit from some orthotics to ensure your walking gait is well aligned. Wearing orthotic inserts can prevent injuries further down the exercise road.

Once you start exercising regularly, you will really start to enjoy it. You will begin to notice the mental benefits right away, and you will soon start to notice the physical changes in your body. Your muscles will become stronger and more defined. These benefits will boost your self-esteem, which will be additional motivation to keep up the exercise habit.

Get the Right Equipment

Make sure you have the right equipment, an outfit you feel good in, and the right pair of footwear. Good footwear is essential. While the outfit won't affect your physical performance, it will affect you psychologically. If you have something to wear that you feel good in, you will be more likely to go do your workout and to actually enjoy it, than if you were wearing something from the bottom of your closet that you dislike. Do not wait until you have "lost those ten pounds" to purchase a pleasing outfit for yourself.

Take Charge of Your Exercise Routine

Exercising with other people can be fun and motivating. However, there are a couple of issues to remember. Make sure they are exercising at the level of intensity that is beneficial to you. As someone with ADHD, you might find to get the maximum mental benefits you may need to workout more intensely than your non-ADHD exercise buddy. Also, be careful you aren't too reliant on them to help motivate you to actually show up for your planned workout sessions. If they can't meet up with you at your regularly scheduled time, there is a high chance you won't go either. Train yourself to go regardless of whether your workout buddy is going or not!!

If you don't like dance or aerobic classes because they require lots of mental energy, you are not alone. Don't feel bad or stupid! Lots of people with ADHD really struggle with these types of classes, so instead do something that comes more naturally to you.

Preparing for Your Exercise Routine

Before you start or increase your exercise program, be sure to get the all-clear from your doctor.

Mental Warm Up
If you do some mental preparation before you start exercising, it will aid in your enjoyment and success with incorporating exercise into your life. A good way to start your preparation is to:

- Brainstorm all the types of exercises you enjoy, and are therefore far more likely to do.
- Consider what actions you need to do before you start.
- Do research to find a local gym, activity club, or online fitness program.

Now consider when in your day you can most easily exercise. For some people it's first thing before work, others it's lunchtime, and yet for others it's after work. When is the best time for you?

What is your plan of action? How many times a week can you commit to this plan? Gradually increase the amount of time you exercise as you build stamina.

Establish Your Baseline Fitness Levels

Take note of where you are now. For example, how many minutes do you work out and/or how much weight can you lift? This will allow you to track your progress. Being able to see how much you are improving will be a great incentive for you to stay motivated!

Congratulate yourself every time you exercise! Mark it on a chart or calendar, or give yourself a gold star. I am not joking! It is surprising how a little time spent keeping track acts as a huge motivational factor.

Set goals for yourself, perhaps running 5K, lifting a certain weight, or touching your toes. Goals help you to see your progress and keep you motivated.

Making It Easy

Make exercise as easy as possible for yourself. For example, have your gym bag packed and ready to go at a moment's notice. If you join a gym or exercise class, join one near your home or work. Have a 'rainy day' plan in place. If you love exercising outside, make sure you have a plan for those rainy or very cold days so you can still keep up with your exercise routine.

Keeping On Track

Don't get bored!

Develop ways to keep your exercise program fun! Set goals for yourself, cross-train, listen to music, motivational audio books or podcasts, and experiment to find out what works best for you.

Buy yourself motivational treats along the way. Perhaps a new workout outfit, an upbeat song, or an online exercise training you've been wanting.

Signing up for a race or competition is a great way to keep motivated and also gives some direction to your training.

It's helpful to have a regular trickle of exercise-related inspiration coming into your life and mind to keep you feeling motivated. There isn't a perfect way to do this, so let your personal preferences guide you. Here are some suggestions!

1. If you love magazines, subscribing to a monthly fitness magazine would be an excellent way to read about new research, inspirational stories, recipes, etc.

2. If you are on Facebook regularly, finding a Facebook group centered around your favorite exercise would be a convenient choice for you.

3. If you love watching YouTube, search for a YouTube channel that resonates with you both in terms of content and presentation style.

4. If you are like me and enjoy podcasts, search for a couple of podcasts that you look forward to listening to each week.

There are lots of options, so don't get overwhelmed. Pick one or possibly two and enjoy those sources without feeling like you are missing out.

ACTIONS

1. Commit to some form of aerobic exercise every day.

2. Follow the suggestions in 'Preparing For Your Exercise Routine' (p. 41-43).

3. Get recommendations of fitness experts and their contact details to have on hand.

4. Pay attention to how you feel on days you don't exercise compared to days that you do. This way you will have concrete evidence for yourself on how great exercise is for you.

5. Having a visual record of when you've exercised helps you to feel motivated. There is a chart to track your progress at the back of this book. You can also download a printable chart from **www.untappedbrilliance.com/chartsfromthebook**

# STEP FOUR

Meditation 101

"Some people think that meditation takes away from physical accomplishment….Most people however, find that meditation creates more time than it takes."

— Peter McWilliams

Meditation seems a contradiction in terms for someone who has ADHD. However, a growing amount of research is showing that meditation is very beneficial for a person with ADHD since it quiets and focuses the mind, and helps with physical relaxation and calmness.

Meditation produces a different state of brain waves from when you are either awake or asleep. Both sides of your brain are active, and your mind and body are connected.

What Are the Benefits of Meditating for an Adult With ADHD?

1. Increases healthy sleep.
2. Decreases mood swings.
3. Increases concentration.
4. Decreases stress.
5. Decreases anxiety.
6. Increases self-confidence.
7. Decreases impulsivity.
8. Increases cognitive functioning.

Meditation can be as complicated or as simple as you want it to be. I will outline the basics here for you. If you become interested in exploring this subject in greater detail, there are many books, retreats and classes you can take to improve your technique and deepen your understanding.

The most important thing is not to feel overwhelmed. You can start practicing meditation today, and it will only take a few minutes. Meditation can be religious, spiritual or purely a technique that helps your ADHD. After trying meditation a few times you will find a technique that works and is meaningful to you. Remember, there is no right or wrong way – whatever works for you is just fine!

9 Steps to Meditating

1. Find somewhere quiet where you will not be disturbed.

2. Sit down. It's not necessary to sit on the floor in a lotus position; you can sit upright in a chair with your two feet planted firmly on the floor. Place your hands in a comfortable position so you

aren't fidgeting. (However, you don't want to make yourself too comfortable and then fall asleep!)

3. Close your eyes.

4. Inhale slowly and deeply.

5. Exhale slowly and deeply.

6. Think about different parts of your body, and concentrate on letting them relax fully (i.e., legs, torso, arms, shoulders, neck, head, etc.)

7. Clear your mind of your thoughts. It is hard to think of absolutely nothing, so here are two suggestions to find a focal point to concentrate on. For every inhalation count "one" and every exhalation count "two": "One, two, one, two." Or, you can think of a word before you start, such as peace, love, or joy and repeat your chosen word slowly throughout the meditation.

8. When other thoughts intrude into your mind, don't get upset with yourself (this is totally natural), just gently bring yourself back to your focal point.

9. Start doing this for 5 minutes a day to begin.

Ideally, it would be great to meditate for 20 minutes; however that can be daunting to begin with, so start with 5 minutes and gradually build up at your own speed to longer sessions. It is more important that your meditation sessions are regular, than the length of time per session.

When Is the Best Time to Meditate?

The best time to meditate would be on waking in the morning before your day starts and you become busy or over-stimulated. It is best to meditate before you have your morning coffee. However, evenings are also good. Some people like to meditate when they get home from work as it helps to de-stress. Others meditate before bedtime as it helps them fall asleep. Experiment and find out what time of day works for you. Some people find it so beneficial that they meditate twice a day.

Meditation Aids

There are meditation apps that can help you meditate. I use the Insight Timer app. It has a timer feature and a beautiful section of interval bells that you can set. It also has guided meditations which can be helpful, especially if you are new to meditation. The Tapping Solution and Calm apps can also be helpful.

How to Approach Meditation When You Have ADHD

Sitting so still and quiet might feel very alien at first and you might feel a sense of confinement. In a society where 'doing' is so highly valued, you might feel it is a waste of time when there are so many more 'productive' things you could be doing. Giving yourself permission to spend this time on yourself is an incredible investment. You will notice the benefits both in the short- and long-term.

Also, you need to be patient. Allowing your body and mind to relax completely is not an easy thing to do. You just need to keep thinking about returning to your focal point and eventually you will achieve a state of total relaxation. Practice makes perfect.

Meditation Can Be a Very Effective Tool for ADHD

Meditation is a very powerful tool for you to use to really help your ADHD symptoms. Try it out and see the benefits for yourself, even if you feel some resistance to it at first.

One of my clients told me that when she meditates first thing in the morning her whole day feels more in control; time travels at a slower speed and she accomplishes more. She is on time or a little early for appointments without obviously trying, and feels a sense of calm inside.

I can visibly see the difference in another client when she does and doesn't meditate. She has a high-powered stressful job and is a single mother with three children. When she practices meditation, she can walk into my office and report many crazy things that are going on in her life, yet she does not seem agitated by any of it. She is calm and is taking everything in her stride. By comparison, in a week when she has not been meditating, her demeanor becomes visibly different and she is much more stressed and agitated.

Meditation can be the first thing you stop doing when life is taking its toll on you, and when time seems short and demands are high. However, it is actually during these times that you benefit the most from meditation. Hopefully, after a short time it will become part of your life, just like sleeping and brushing your teeth. Even if you have progressed up to 20 minutes, and can meditate for that length of time, if time is short, go back to 5 minutes. Five minutes is always better than no minutes. Even if you stop meditating for a number of days or even weeks, do not despair, give up, or feel bad about yourself. Simply start again!

Pay attention to the benefits of meditation for you. What results are you noticing? Once you start to see the results yourself, it will be easier for you to sit and take time to do this daily. It can become an enjoyable ritual for you, one that you look forward to.

ACTIONS

1. Think what time of day you would like to start to meditate.

2. Decide which room would be best for you to meditate in.

3. Follow the nine steps to meditating. (Optional: download a meditation app to help you)

4. Pay attention to the personal benefits that you notice.

5. Record your progress in your "Untapped Brilliance Binder." You can download a printable tracking chart here:
www.untappedbrilliance.com/chartsfromthebook
(There is also a starter tracking chart at the back of this book.)

STEP FIVE

Get a Good Nights Sleep

"There is only one thing people like that is good for them; a good night's sleep"

— Edgar Watson Howe

Sleep is the cornerstone of all the other steps. Without sleep, not only are you unable to function well, but you are also less likely to be able to do the other ten steps since you do not have the mental or physical energy to carry them out. When you are not able to get a good night's sleep, you experience many unpleasant symptoms, many of which mirror your ADHD symptoms, such as:

1. Anxiety
2. Difficulty concentrating
3. Fatigue
4. Forgetfulness
5. Headaches
6. Hyperactivity
7. Increased distractibility

While getting a good night's sleep minimizes your ADHD symptoms and allows you to function at your best, a large percentage of the ADHD adult population have problems sleeping. The most common problem is not being able to fall asleep but other issues include waking up numerous times during the night and not being able to wake up easily in the morning.

Everyone needs different amounts of sleep. However, initially you should aim for 8 hours. So if you have to get up at 7:00 am, then an 11:00 pm bedtime would be perfect for you.

All the steps in this book will aid in a good night's sleep. Your body needs nutrients while it is sleeping, as well as when you are awake, so eating healthy food aids sleep. Exercise enhances sleep, as does meditation. An organized home promotes mental calmness and will aid in falling asleep easily since there are no visible distractions. Having developed routines and systems, you can be confident as you hop into bed that you have taken care of everything and you will have less on your mind as you are falling asleep.

Why Is Sleeping Hard If You Have ADHD?

Medication
Some medications for ADHD, particularly if taken later on in the day, make falling asleep very difficult.

Hyperfocus
Getting hyperfocused late in the evening might mean losing track of time and bedtime is forgotten.

Brain Is Working Overtime
Being unable to slow down your brain in order to relax and fall asleep.

Worrying
Worrying about the day's events or chores left unfinished.

Top 12 Tips to Get a Good Night's Sleep

1. Think of a Realistic Bedtime and Go to Bed at that Same Time Each Night

When you do this, your body starts to get into a routine and falls into a habit of feeling sleepy at the same time each day. If you currently fall asleep at 2:00 am, but would like to fall asleep at 10:00 pm each night, then 10:00 pm actually isn't a *realistic* bedtime for you at the moment. If you tried to do this, it might work for a few nights, but then you would face resistance and feel like a failure. The better option is to start slowly and build up a pattern of success. Set your new bedtime for 1:00 am; then work back to 12:00 midnight; then 11:00 pm and finally to 10:00 pm. It might take a few weeks or even months, but when you get there you will feel really proud.

When you have had a good night's sleep you feel more energetic, alive, positive and creative. Even if you are really enjoying an activity and do not want to go to bed, remember how good you feel on days when you are well-rested. This should act as a motivating factor in getting you to bed on time.

2. Wake Up at the Same Time Each Morning, Even on the Weekends

Waking up is typically quite difficult for someone with ADHD usually because they have had difficulty falling asleep the night before, or have woken several times during the night or went to bed too late.

Even if you didn't go to bed at your realistic bedtime and feel like sleeping through the alarm clock, still get up when you hear it ring no matter how hard it is.

The first few days will be especially difficult but the more consistent you are at getting up at the same time each morning the easier it will become. And, you will also find it a lot easier to fall asleep at your proper bedtime as well!

One trick to getting up on time is to place your alarm clock away from your bed so that you have to physically get out of bed to switch it off. In addition, you could also have a radio that is set to come on a few minutes before the alarm goes off. You will be gently aware of the radio playing in the background and then the noise of the alarm will not be such a surprise.

3. Do Not Nap During the Day

When you are trying to develop a habit of going to bed at a consistent hour napping during the day could sabotage your efforts. If you suffer from insomnia, experts believe napping is not a good thing for you to do. If you are feeling a little sleepy during the day, take a walk, jump up and down on the spot, or phone a friend, but don't take a nap.

4. Exercise on a Regular Basis but Not Too Close to Bedtime

Physical exercise helps to make your body ready to fall asleep at night, and your sleep will be deeper than someone who doesn't exercise. However, if you exercise too close to bedtime, then your heart will still be beating too rapidly and it will actually prevent you from falling asleep.

5. Do Not Drink Caffeine After 3:00 PM

It is a stimulant so it will keep you awake.

6. Do Not Smoke or Drink Alcohol

Alcohol might help you fall asleep initially but then it increases the chance of you waking up in the night. Nicotine is a stimulant and will therefore also prevent you from falling asleep.

7. Take Up Meditation and Practice It for a Few Minutes in the Evening

This is a great way to calm your mind down after a busy day. Refer to the meditation chapter to learn more

8. Create Your Own Bedtime Routine

Just as a child responds well to a bedtime routine, adults do too. The bedtime routine sends messages to your body and mind that you are winding down. Your routine might include a bath (which causes your body temperature to first increase and then fall, which facilitates sleep), a cup of herbal tea, or a glass of milk (the calcium in the milk has a calming effect).

9. Turn Off Your TV and Computer 2 Hours Before Bedtime

This helps your brain activity to slow down before bed, and decreases the chances of getting hyperfocused and going to bed later than you would ideally like.

You can use this time to write down any worries or actions you need to do tomorrow. Writing down your worries downloads them from your mind and helps you to 'turn off' the mental chatter in your brain.

10. Designate Your Bedroom for Sleep and Sex Only

Do not have a TV, computer or do any work in your bedroom. Don't use your bedroom as a 'hang out' place or to do lots of activities. This can make falling asleep very difficult as it conditions your mind that the bedroom is a place for other actions rather than sleep.

11. Try Using Background Sounds

If you find you need some noise to aid you in falling asleep, then have a fan, radio, or a white noise machine humming in the background.

12. Sweet dreams!

ACTIONS

1. Follow the top 12 tips to get a good night's sleep.

2. If you do take medication for your ADHD and think that might be a reason why you are having trouble sleeping, talk to your doctor.

3. Think what lifestyle changes from the top 12 tips apply to you and how and when you will go about making those changes. For example, move a TV or ironing board out of the bedroom, and create your own bedtime routine.

STEP SIX

Thrive in Your Environment

"Out of clutter find simplicity"

— Albert Einstein

Steps 1 to 5 were focused on caring for your physical body. Now we are broadening the focus to include your environment.

How would you describe your home? Clean? Dirty? Stylish? Messy? Tidy? In *feng shui* it is said that your environment is an outer reflection of what is taking place inside you, and that your physical environment has a direct effect on your health, emotions and energy. Research has also shown that there are many negative effects of being in an untidy and cluttered environment.

What Is Clutter?

Clutter is anything that is lying around your home in an inappropriate place. Clutter is not necessarily junk or rubbish (although it can be). Clutter can be very nice objects, but if they're in the wrong place, then they become plain old clutter.

Anything that you haven't used in two years, or that no longer reflects you as you are today, can be considered clutter. For example, if you play tennis on a weekly basis, then it's great that you have lots of tennis balls, rackets and cute outfits, because it's your hobby. If you haven't played for 10 years, then these things are now clutter. Books that do not reflect your interests anymore, even if they look impressive on your shelves, such as the classics, can be removed. Children's toys, clothes and equipment, once they have grown out of them, can be removed from your home. Any cooking tools or gadgets that don't get used often can be removed as well. These things are all clutter, and are crowding you and affecting your mental health.

Clutter can also be items that are broken or outdated. Anything that is broken and you haven't got round to fixing yet, is considered clutter. If you upgrade an item, such as a TV or cell phone, then get rid of the old one, even if it is still working.

Some things have special memories, such as an outfit you wore to an occasion that you really enjoyed, a gift from someone you love, or a holiday souvenir. You don't actually need the outfit to remember that special day, or the gift to know that someone loves you. If you are no longer actually using these items, then they can be discarded.

Why clutter and keeping a tidy home is such a hard task for people with ADHD

Keeping a tidy environment involves patience for doing the often dull and unexciting tasks such as putting items away, or making decisions and prioritizing your space. All of these are challenging for people with ADHD. Clutter builds up gradually, day by day. Every time you start something and get distracted and move to the next activity, the items from the first activity are left lying around, whether they are items from your fridge, brief case or a hobby you were working on. Procrastination also aids in clutter accumulation. Every time you say, "I will get to it later," a little more clutter is added. The negative effects of clutter actually exacerbate your ADHD symptoms, whereas a tidy environments lessens them.

Effects of Clutter – Negatives vs. Positives of Clearing It

1. Attention, Focus and Clarity
Being in a cluttered and messy environment fosters distraction, as your mind is always jumping from one thing to another. "Oh, I must mail that birthday card" or "I really need to unpack that bag" and "That load of clothes from the dryer needs putting away". All these things make concentration very difficult.

The positives of living in a beautiful, tidy and organized house with minimal distractions are that you are able to think clear thoughts. Also, even though you have ADHD, you are giving yourself a much better chance of being able to focus on the task at hand.

2. Time
You are short on time because it takes so much longer to do things when you are jumping over piles of dirty laundry and dodging boxes. Plus it takes you longer to find things you need in order to do anything.

You may feel shy to invite people into your home because of the mess. Or you don't feel you should be going out because there is so much work to be done to clean your home. Both of these issues result in you withdrawing socially. Equally, if the house is really untidy, it can affect family time as well. For example, if the dining table is so full of clutter that you can't eat there, you end up eating on trays in front of the TV.

Life dreams are put on hold because you think you will work

on your goals 'once the house is clear.' I have seen clients who have been trying for years and years to clear their house. It wouldn't take years and years in human hours to achieve a clear living space, but because the task isn't pleasant and it provokes anxiety, procrastination sets in and their life is put on hold.

After decluttering, rather than spending your free time decluttering, or feeling bad when you do something other than decluttering, you can now enjoy your hobbies with a sense of freedom.

You no longer withdraw socially because of clutter. The people in your life are welcome in your home anytime.

There is nothing stopping you to reach your goals - the sky is the limit.

3. Feelings of General Well-Being
Being surrounded by so much disorganization and not being able to find things is stressful, and can make you grumpy, irritable and anxious. Clutter in our physical environment causes a cluttered mind, and a cluttered mind is not in the right mental state to take power over the mess. You don't know where anything is and it takes you ages to find something. You feel out of control and very disorganized.

On the other hand, feelings of calm and peace grow in a tidy, organized environment. There are no distractions and both the body and mind are calm.

4. Control Over Your Life
You feel overwhelmed because there is so much to do and you don't know where to start. After decluttering, you feel happy that this worrisome weight is no longer in your life. The clutter is no longer in control of you.

5. Energy and Mental Health
Your energy gets sucked out of you when you walk into a room full of

clutter and tiredness sweeps over you. Research shows that clutter, particularly when it is on the floor, creates feelings of depression.

Energy is increased after decluttering because it is not being sucked out of you by the clutter.

6. Self-Esteem

This is a 'Catch 22' situation. Low self-esteem is manifested by having a messy home, and if you feel bad about yourself, you won't take the time to make your living environment pleasant. Even when you are not physically in your home environment, you think about it and it mentally weighs you down.

You will have a greater respect for yourself because you created this clutter-free environment for yourself. You will no longer have the negative voice in your head saying, "You can't do that! You can't even keep your own house tidy!" Your house will be tidy and you will feel a sense of pride about that.

Because your living environment is an extension of you, and it is now clean and tidy, you will have a greater sense of self-respect. People in your life will also have greater respect for you.

7. Space

No matter how big your home is, clutter invades your space, making it much smaller than it needs to be.

The benefits of having fewer belongings are manifold. Besides all the mental benefits, there are also practical reasons such as finding things more quickly.

8. Money

Money is wasted because it is easier to buy something that you already own than to try and find it in the clutter. Bills are lost and not paid on time and extra fees are incurred. In extreme cases, mice and bugs can start to take up residence in your home, and then you have to pay to have them exterminated. You might keep buying new organizing tools, as these items promise to be the answer to your problem, yet they never seem to help.

After decluttering, you won't have to spend extra money on purchasing items you already have, because you can readily find them.

Where to Start?

Your ultimate goal is to create a wonderful, clean, and organized feeling in your home. Even if you have never been tidy and as a child you always had a messy bedroom, you can declutter your home. It won't happen overnight, but if you do it you will feel really proud of yourself.

Decluttering List
Grab a piece of paper and walk around your house and write down all areas that need to be 'decluttered'. Break the items down individually rather than write 'the bedroom' or 'the whole house'. For example, write "Clean and organize the 4 drawers in the chest of drawers in the bedroom," or "Clean and organize the cabinet under the sink."

Decluttering Rules
Create some rules for yourself. For example, if you haven't used the item in question in a year, then it's time to let it go. Also, use the phrase "If in doubt, chuck it out" to help declutter your home.

Decluttering Time
Decide on how much time to spend per week on your project. I recommend 15 minutes every day. Set your timer and work for 15 minutes until it goes off.

If done every day, you will build up momentum and you won't forget to do it, since it will have become a daily habit. A lot can be achieved in 15 minutes, and even if you have had a busy day, you can still find 15 minutes for decluttering. Plus, you will experience peace of mind, because every time you think about your cluttered home with a sinking heart, you'll know that it is being taken care of and that you are on top of it ... 15 minutes at a time!

Weekend Routine
In addition to the daily 15 minutes, spend one hour on weekends, either on Saturday or Sunday, to continue the decluttering process. Break the hour up into four segments of 15 minutes each and use your timer to time yourself. This is when you have some extra time and it will help to make more headway into decluttering your home.

Don't Overdo It
If you genuinely feel inspired to do more on any given day, then go ahead and spend another 15 minutes, or as many more minutes as you want. The important thing is to not burn out. Don't spend 12 hours one day and then not be able to face decluttering for another year.

Focus Only on De-Cluttering
When you are working for those 15 minutes, do nothing but declutter. Keep moving! It is very easy to get side-tracked when you find something interesting that you haven't seen for ages (e.g., finding a letter and starting to read it, etc.). However, put the item aside and look at it once the 15 minutes are up.

Space for Everything and Everything in Its Place
You need to create a place for everything. By throwing away and/or donating items not used anymore, you are making room in your cupboards for items you actually do use. Let's take the kitchen for

example. If you get rid of all the gadgets you don't use, and all the food that is out of date, then Abracadabra! There is more room in the cupboards! When everything has a home, it is easy to use an item and put it away afterwards, plus it is easier to find things. This will make you feel happy and calm whenever you open a cupboard and and do not have things fall out on you.

Positive Self-Talk

As you are working away, remember to tell yourself positive messages. It's easy to talk to yourself in a negative way, beating yourself up about not doing this sooner, finding an unpaid bill, or something that you couldn't find and ended up buying a replacement. If negative messages start to pop into your mind, gently tell yourself, "It's OK! I'm doing well and I'm making progress." You are making a huge step in your life, and it won't go without rewards, because very soon you will start to see the positive effect it has on your life. While clearing clutter can be boring, tiring and anxiety provoking, it can also be freeing and energizing. If negative feelings sneak up on you, remind yourself why you are doing this and how great you will feel afterward.

What To Do With Belongings You Don't Want?

Don't feel guilty about throwing things out or giving them a new home. It is not a waste. It's a waste to let the things go on clogging up your home and having a negative effect on you.

Find a charity that really means something to you. It makes letting go of your items much easier when it's a charity that speaks to you. For example, a children's hospital for your unused toys, your local library for books, a women's shelter for clothes, the Salvation Army, or perhaps another charity. There are many great charities out there, where your possessions will be put to good use. Knowing this can aid you in letting go of your belongings.

You could sell some of your stuff on eBay, Facebook Marketplace, etc. The caveat here is only do this if you think you can. Don't do it out of guilt. If the thought of spending time researching how to sell stuff on the internet is overwhelming or you have other concerns, take everything to your charity's drop-off point and get rid of it. If, however, it inspires you and excites you, then selling things would be a great way to clear space and get extra money.

If you are really stuck over an item, a good way to decide whether or not you should get rid of it is to hold it in both hands, and see how it feels. If you feel happy and positive about the item, it's a keeper. If you feel the item makes you sad, or sucks energy out of you, then it's definitely time to let it go.

Don't save your clutter to give to people you know unless they have actually told you that they would like it. Chances are they have their own clutter to deal with. While it is easier for you to give it to another person, you might not actually be helping them.

If you are scared to throw out a pile of newspaper and magazine articles because you want to learn more about the subject, then write them down on a list (article topic and newspaper/magazine date) so that you can do further research when you have time in the future. If you don't want to throw out some old clothes because they might come back in style, then remind yourself that the new style will likely be slightly different, and the old clothes may not fit.

Staying Motivated

Check Off Completed Items
Every time you complete a task on your To Do List, check it off, and keep this list. This is important because it is easy to forget how much work you have actually done, and a quick glance over the list will make you feel good about yourself and make you want to do more.

Before and After Photos

Take before and after photos. It is easy to do with your phone camera. Take photos of the room you are working on before you touch anything. Then take photos along the way to monitor your progress. You will be surprised at how fast you forget how things used to be, and the photos will help you to monitor your progress and give you a sense of satisfaction.

Treats

Another way to keep motivated is to buy little organizing treats along the way (perhaps a label maker, organizing boxes, spice racks, shoe racks, pen holders, folders, etc.). Not only are these items very practical, but they can also act as incentives. Let's take the example of a label maker. If this will inspire you to file your documents and label the files neatly, then it's a really good investment.

Organizing boxes can come in many pretty colors or very practical ones, and they are good to store similar objects together. Buy these treats as you go along, because before you start the de-cluttering, you don't really know what you will need.

Anti-cluttering Tactics

Once you have cleared an area, put something pretty on top of the clean spaces such as a picture frame, a vase of flowers, or anything else that is appealing to your eye. This stops you from putting new piles of papers on the clean surface. To a person who is used to clutter, a freshly cleared and clean surface looks so tempting to pop a pile of papers on. However, if it has something attractive on it, that can make you stop and think just long enough to stop and go file those papers where they belong.

When you have attractive things in your environment, it can also be an incentive to keep it tidy and clean. For example, if it's time for a new bookcase or new bedding, now would be a great time to invest in those items. It is much easier to declutter an environment where there are lovely pieces of furniture, since it feels like the space deserves to be tidy. If you feel guilty about spending money, you can always use any cash you made from selling your old items.

How To Keep Your Environment Clean and Tidy

Daily Maintenance
There are certain areas of your home that will require daily maintenance. For example, the kitchen, (tidying and washing dishes), the bathroom (a quick wipe over the shower, toilet and sink), and bedroom (making your bed, putting your clothes away), the living room (picking up dishes and snack wrappers after the evening is over), etc. When you get into the habit of doing these things each and every day, they will soon become second nature, and it will feel strange to go to bed having not done them.

To make this more fun for yourself, have a race against your timer and see how many rooms you can do in 15 minutes.

A lot of my clients have great success using the book *Sink Reflections* by Marla Cilley, the Flylady. She advocates the use of routines in the morning and evening to maintain a clean and tidy home. She is also a big fan of the kitchen timer. If you aren't sure how to actually clean, then Jeff Campbell and the 'Clean Team' have a great book teaching you how to clean your home in record -breaking time called *Speed Cleaning*. The book is old, but good cleaning techniques don't date!

After reading this chapter, I am sure you will agree that there are many benefits to having a clean and tidy home. It will depend on the condition of your home how long it takes to declutter it, but you will start to feel and see the benefits after the first 15 minutes.

ACTIONS

1. Grab a piece of paper and walk around your house and write down all the areas that need to be decluttered. Break the areas down. There are charts in the back of the book to help you, or get printables at **www.untappedbrilliance.com/chartsfromthebook**

2. Create your own rules. If it hasn't been used in the last year, throw it out.

3. Spend 15 minutes a day sorting and throwing out your clutter.

4. Spend one hour each weekend sorting and throwing out your clutter.

5. Reward yourself often for a job well done!

STEP SEVEN

Set Goals That Excite You

"You are never given a dream without also being given the power to make it true."

— **Richard Bach**

Now that you are taking vitamins and organizing your home, you might think, "This is great, but what's it all for?"

That's where goals come in. Goals give small actions a greater meaning. This framework brings everything together.

How do you feel when you hear the word 'goals'? For many people with ADHD, it makes them feel stressed. They believe that goals don't work for them or they feel overwhelmed.

Good news: you are better at goals than you think! You might even have goals you are working toward now but you have not formally called them goals.

Cast your mind over your life so far. What have you accomplished? Those things were, probably, goals that you worked towards reaching.

Perhaps you wanted to meet a life partner. You wrote your dating profile and posted it on a dating app. You replied to text messages, bought a new outfit or two, and went out on dates. These are all steps towards achieving your goal.

Your goals don't have to be grand or lofty. Although, they absolutely can be! Whether it's writing a book or running a marathon, decluttering your house or learning to manage your ADHD, the important thing is to set a goal that excites you.

Sometimes a goal takes longer than you wanted. Sometimes there are setbacks that you didn't anticipate. Rather than being critical of yourself, when this happens, simply ask, "What have I learned?" and, "What would I do differently next time?"

10 Reasons Why Goals Are Helpful if You Have ADHD

1. Having a goal gives you daily direction, focus, and energy.
2. It is easier to prioritize tasks when you are working towards a goal.
3. Goals help you make decisions, even if you usually find decision-making difficult.
4. You'll feel accomplished at the end of each day because you completed tasks. Without a goal, it's easy to jump from one task to the next without finishing them.
5. The tasks you need to do to reach your goal might not be enjoyable, yet you are motivated to do them because they are part of your bigger picture.
6. Your confidence increases. When you take action and accomplish something, big or small, you feel good about yourself.
7. Working on your goals helps you to understand the passage of time.

8. You develop an understanding of how long tasks take you, so you get good at planning.

9. You start to trust yourself to do things that are important to you. You stop feeling like your achievements were a 'fluke' because you know how you did them and could do them again.

10. By setting external goals, you develop internal characteristics and skills that stay with you long after the goals have been achieved.

For printable charts to help you with your goal setting, go to **www.untappedbrilliance.com/chartsfromthebook**

How to Define Your "Big Picture"

What would you do if you couldn't fail? If money were no object? What is important to you? Deep down, you probably know but perhaps are shy to acknowledge it even to yourself. Also, beware of any inner voice that replies, 'That will never happen.' Be brave and don't censor yourself.

"Big Picture" Exercise

Close your eyes and envision yourself being lifted up from where you are in this moment, and being transported high above the clouds. From your new vantage point, you can see the whole world rotating. It looks like a big, blue and green globe, as once, twice and then a third time it spins slowly round. It's an amazing sight and one that changes your perspective and makes you realize anything is possible.

Before you return to earth, you can make decisions on what you want in your life. Decide what qualities and traits you have now that you didn't before, as well as who is important in your life, and the physical possessions you own.

Now you are traveling back through the clouds, but this time you have a choice. You can choose which country, city and area of town you live in. You can choose any place in the world, not just the one you were living in before this happened. You can choose what type of home you are living in, how big it is, the type of furniture, the car or cars in your driveway. Literally everything is your choice.

Now you have landed back in your new home. How does it feel? How do you feel? Do you feel happy? Is your life full of fun and fulfillment? What does it look like? Describe your typical day.

Are you healthier? Do you exercise an amount you are pleased with? What foods do you eat? Do you have the same hairstyle? What type of clothes are you wearing? What qualities do you have now that you didn't have before?

Who is there with you? Is your partner there? Are there children in the picture? Do you hang out with the same friends, and/or new ones? What is it about any new friends that you like? How do you spend your leisure time? Do you throw parties? Visit a different country every year? Own a holiday home? What hobbies do you do?

What work do you do? Do you work from home, or have a workplace somewhere else? Do you work for yourself, or work for someone else? If someone else, what are they like? Which charities do you support? How many pets do you have? What sorts of activities do you do with your extended family? What skills and character traits do you have?

Have you reached your full potential? What would you like to accomplish one day? For example, learn to draw, go to Australia, do a parachute jump, learn to speak in public, make 'x' amount of money, retire at 50, learn to play a musical instrument, meet your hero, have your book on the New York Times best seller list, etc.

Now get out your 'Untapped Brilliance Binder' (p. 17) and write down everything that you saw for yourself. This is your blueprint or map that you can make your decisions with. Everyone wants to feel fulfilled and happy and share their life with wonderful people. How people feel fulfilled and happy is different for everyone.

By completing this exercise, you will have broken the mental barriers of what you 'should' do. You will have written down what you would love to be, have, and do.

The very act of writing them down makes them more likely to happen. Attitude is everything. BELIEVE you can achieve all of the above and you will!

Dream Big!

The bigger you dare to dream, the more inspired you will feel. For example, if your dream is to own a house on the water, with a wooden walkway and a place to moor your boat, that vision will inspire you every day and excite and motivate you to take action to realize it.

However, if you were being 'realistic,' your negative voice would not allow you to think like that. It might say to you, "That would never happen and you would be better off to get a three-bedroom house in the suburbs." That might be your idea of a prison, but that is the 'realistic' goal. If that doesn't excite you, or if in fact that frightens you, you wont be able to conjure up the motivation to take action. You might then think to yourself, "Well, if I can't even do what it takes to get a house in the suburbs, what chance do I have for my dream house?" However, it doesn't work like that. Don't settle. The more exciting your goals are to you, the more you are willing to break out of your comfort zone and do things to achieve them.

Sometimes it can be disheartening thinking of everything you want. It may feel daunting when you look at where you are right now, and the difference between the two places feels so big that it could never happen. It is helpful to see the big picture to get inspired and to get the internal drive to achieve it. But if at times it becomes overwhelming, gently bring yourself back to the task at hand and simply concentrate on that for now. This will diminish the anxiety and feelings of being overwhelmed.

Create a Two-ish Year Plan

Using the information from your 'Big Picture' exercise, create a two-ish year plan! Although we often hear about five year plans, two-ish years is a helpful time frame when you have ADHD. Thinking five years into the future might make you feel anxious or overwhelmed. Plus, having a fixed deadline can feel constraining, or you might feel that you have failed if you don't reach your goal by that time.

Thinking and planning two years ahead is easier because it is tangible and less abstract. The 'ish' means approximately. Because there is some flexibility in the timeline, you can't fail. You are setting yourself up for success. Also, the term 'ish' is informal, which can help if you are a perfectionist and think your goals and plans have to be 'just right.'

When you write your plan, you don't need to know every single step. Just write down what you do know at the moment. The other steps will become clear once you make a start.

What Are the Elements Required for Goal Setting?
Every goal should have:

1. A timeframe. Eight-week timeframes are helpful; the next section will teach you about this.

2. An element of precision, so you know when you have achieved it. 'Exercise more' is vague. 'Run a 5k race' is specific.

3. A target that stretches your capabilities, but that is realistic to achieve. It would be a definite 'stretch' to set a goal to lose 100 pounds, but it would not be realistic to plan to lose all of it in the next three months!

4. A daily action. What is one daily action that you could do to achieve your goal?

5. An emotion. How will you feel when you have achieved this?
6. A reward. How will you reward yourself when you have achieved this goal?

When you write your goals, you take your focus off of the rather daunting 'big picture' and focus on a specific detail that is very achievable.

But it's also good to remind yourself of the big picture on a daily basis to help take your mind off the drudgery and stay excited. For example, if you are training for a marathon, waking up at 5:00 am isn't always fun. If you focus on that detail and the hardship of leaving your warm bed, then it might be very difficult to go out training. However, reminding yourself of the big picture motivates you to keep working towards the very good feelings that will come when you have accomplished your goal!

Set Eight-Week Goals

Work in time chunks of eight weeks. Eight weeks gives you enough time to get things done. Because the finish line is always in sight, you'll feel a helpful (not stressful) sense of urgency to take action.

Go to **www.untappedbrilliance.com/chartsfromthebook** for a worksheet to help you lay out your first eight-week plan.

From your vision, pick three things you would like to work on. Keep in mind that you are working through this book with actions in it. Do not be too ambitious with your choices. You might feel inspired in the moment, however, if you take on too much it could result in feeling overwhelmed and despondent later.

Your first eight-week plan might include:

1. Spend one hour a week researching your dream home.
2. Work on one daily routine so it becomes a habit.
3. Host a party to show off your new decluttered home.

If you finish all your goals before the eight weeks are up, check your 'Master List' (p. 86) for tasks (one at a time). Every eight weeks set new goals for yourself relating to your 'Big Picture.'

How to Stay Inspired

Visualization is very powerful. Visualizing your success will help you to stay focused during the not so fun times. If you are studying and it's boring and hard and you would rather be doing a hundred and one other things, then visualize yourself dressed in your graduation gown, while going up on stage and being handed your certificate. Or picture having a graduation party with all your family and friends there to celebrate your success. How will you feel? For each visualization, be aware of your emotions. Linking positive emotions to the visualization will have an even more powerful effect.

If you are training for a marathon, you might visualize crossing the finish line and feeling exhilarated at achieving this wonderful accomplishment. People with ADHD are good at daydreaming, so this should come easily to you!

Some ways to stay on track are to watch inspiring movies, or read inspiring books or biographies. The human spirit is very strong and resilient and when we watch or read about some of the challenges people have faced and lived to tell their story, it gives us strength to continue on our path. Find quotes that inspire and motivate you. Write them out and put them in places you will see them, such as on your desk at work.

Don't get scared about the future. The things we worry about almost never happen, and when we worry about all the possibilities of bad things happening, it takes away our strength to deal with what is going on in our life today. Just focus on what you are doing right now. You can always do what you have planned for today, realizing that tomorrow is another day and you will have everything you will need for tomorrow when it arrives. If you find yourself worrying, which is a trait of ADHD sufferers, gently bring yourself back into the moment. Focus on what you are doing that very second.

You might be lying in bed with your cat on your chest. At that moment, nothing bad is happening. If you imagine a bad thing, it is in your head and chances are it will never happen. If it actually does, know you will be able to handle it.

Create a Treasure Map or Vision Board

Go through a selection of magazines and pick out pictures that represent what you want in your life. If you want a big house in the country, then find a picture of that. If you want to find a great life partner, find a picture that represents that image to you.

Once you have found your pictures and arranged them on a big piece of cardboard, find a space in your home for it to hang, somewhere where you will see it every day. Your bedroom is a good place since it is private, but it can also be a room that you see often. Whenever you see these pictures, it sends a message to your subconscious and reminds you what you are working towards.

Some of the things can be very specific. For example, if there is an exact type of car you would like, find a picture of that exact model and post it on your board. For other items that you would like in your life it might not be possible to find an exact image. For a goal such as 'inner happiness,' you can just find a picture that represents that emotion for you.

A treasure map is a powerful tool as it acts as a constant reminder of your dreams. Every time you catch a glimpse of it, it sends a message to your subconscious mind of what you are working towards.

ACTIONS

1. Carry out the 'Big Picture Exercise' so you know what you are working towards.
   You can find charts for this and other actions in this chapter in the Charts section of this book (p. 143). For printable charts, go to **www.untappedbrilliance.com/chartsfromthebook**

2. Create your two-ish year plan!

3. Write your eight-week goals, with do-able actions. For more information on what a 'do-able action' is, visit this blog post: **www.untappedbrilliance.com/doable**

4. Take at least one action a day towards your goal. Even the smallest action brings you one step closer to your goal, and keeps the momentum going!

5. Create a treasure map or vision board and mount it in a place where you can see it every day.

6. Give yourself treats and rewards at certain key points. Make a list of all your favorite things and then use them as rewards along your path. These act as incentives and as a reinforcement that you are doing well.

7. Believe in yourself: No matter what ... you can achieve your goal!

8. To learn more about ADHD and goals go to this article: **www.untappedbrilliance.com/goals**

STEP EIGHT

Staying on Track

"Let him who would enjoy a good future waste none of his present"
— **Roger Babson**

Now that you know what your goals are, it is important to stay on track and work towards those goals. Time management, routines, and anti-procrastination techniques will all assist you with staying on track.

When we hear the phrase 'time management' we generally think in terms of one-day chunks. We focus on how to manage the hours and minutes in each day and the appointments and meetings that need to be attended to during those hours.

However, the consequence of focusing on only one day at a time is you will spend a lot of time putting out fires. The days go by quickly and turn into months, then into years. To fulfill your potential, it is important to take control of the passage of time and not let this happen to you. You have already identified your goals. Now we will focus on day-to-day life, to ensure that it is productive and stress-free, while keeping an eye on the future so that your goals are achieved as well.

Time management is a vital aspect to functioning well in the world, but it poses problems for people with ADHD. It involves planning, not getting distracted from the plan, making approximations of how long each activity takes, transitioning from one activity to another, and awareness of the passage of time. All of this can be problematic for people with ADHD.

Use a Calendar

The first step to staying on track is to use a calendar/planner. If you don't already use one, start today! Even if you haven't been able to use one in the past, keep an open mind. This chapter will help you!

When choosing a calendar or planner, choose one with a date layout that is appealing to you. If you want to be able to see your week in advance, get one with this feature. If you like to see only one page for one day, then get one that is laid out this way. Select one that you find attractive and pleasing to your eye. It will make a difference. For help on selecting the best calendar for your ADHD brain, go to **www.untappedbrilliance.com/yourcalendar**.

The second step is to actually use it! For every appointment you have or make, enter it into your calendar. If you go to work and know you are going to be there from 9:00 am to 5:00 pm, then it's not necessary to enter 'work' in these time slots unless you find it helpful. Do, however, enter any appointments you might have at lunchtime or in the evening in your calendar. If your work is made up of appointments, then enter those in, plus the telephone number of the person you are visiting, so if anything comes up, you have all the information you need close at hand.

If you have an appointment at 1:00 pm on Thursday the 12th of June, find the corresponding date and in the 1:00 pm time section, enter "1:00 pm: Appointment with Mr. Smith." Always include the name, in case you forget, then the person's telephone number.

Five Keys to Using Your Calendar

1. Don't leave home without it.

2. Don't make an appointment with anyone without first checking if you already have something booked in that same time slot.

3. The minute you make an appointment, enter it in (your calendar/planner will already be at the ready from step two). This way you won't forget to do it later. Always use only the calendar to write down/enter appointments, rather than on odd scraps of paper that can get lost.

4. Check your calendar before going to bed to see what you have planned for the next day.

5. If you can't remember when you wake up what your day looks like, check your calendar to refresh your memory.

Ideally, you should use your calendar and view it as an asset in your life rather than as a ball and chain. One of my clients loves his vacations a great deal. Not because he gets to rest or see a different part of the world, but because he doesn't have to use his calendar. If you feel like that, then it's not the healthy relationship we are striving for! We want you to feel your calendar is a useful tool that aids you in your life so you can be at places that you said you would be, on time. It allows you to feel in control of your life.

Create A Daily 'To Do' List

As a supplement to your calendar, always create a list of things to do that day and keep it near your calendar. These are not appointments with other people, so they aren't written in a specific time slot.

The benefit of this list being separate from the calendar is if you aren't able to get the full list of things done that day, it is still a useful list for the next day.

At the top of the list you could write something positive like "Today will be a good day if I get 1._____, 2._____, and 3._____ done." These could be items from any of the categories on your Master List (see p. 86), or they could be daily living tasks such as doing grocery shopping or picking up your dry cleaning.

Try not to be too ambitious when writing your list. It's better to get everything on the list accomplished rather than to write too much down and then feel bad about yourself for not doing everything. Or to feel so overwhelmed when you see the list that you don't even start any of the items.

Don't Procrastinate!

Procrastination is a deeply entrenched habit, and reasons for procrastination are multifaceted. People with ADHD are known for their distractibility, so when doing a task and something else more enjoyable or less painful or more interesting comes up, the task in hand gets exchanged for the more interesting one. Using your timer and saying, "I will keep on task until the timer goes off" is a helpful idea.

The techniques outlined in this chapter will definitely help any procrastination habits. Having routines provides structure and causes less mental debate about whether you should do or not do a task. Procrastination also occurs when you have tasks to do that you are not good at or you don't have the skills to do. Delegating those tasks that you are not good at to someone else who is more qualified takes the pressure off you. Setting personal deadlines and giving yourself treats are other ways to beat procrastination.

Fear is another reason tasks don't get done. For example, you may have some phone calls to make to the bank and other businesses that you don't particularly enjoy dealing with, and you keep putting off making the calls. It's fear that is making you procrastinate these tasks.

There is a wonderful book by Susan Jeffers called *Feel the Fear and Do It Anyway*. The message here is that everyone experiences fear, but people who are successful feel the fear and go ahead anyway and do the thing that seems scary. I'm sure that there is a high likelihood that the first man who walked on the moon felt a bit scared before actually doing it, but he went ahead and did it anyway. Procrastination requires some self-reflection, to work out what is causing you to procrastinate and why. Once you know the reason why you are procrastinating for any task, you have identified the monster and then it doesn't seem so scary.

Create an Anti-procrastination List

Your anti-procrastination list is a list of everything that you would like/need to catch up on.

Start creating this list now. Walk through every room of your home for inspiration. You don't need to write items that need decluttering (those are on your decluttering list already), but do write down things that you have been meaning to do and haven't gotten around to doing yet.

For example, in the hallway you might notice a pile of unopened mail, so write, "Open mail." From there comes other actions such as "Pay bills," "Reply to wedding invitation" or "File taxes for the last four years." There might be a clock in the living room that needs a new battery, the fish tank needs cleaning, there are dental appointments to make or an annual checkup for your cat. Keep walking around and writing EVERTYHING that needs to be done. In your bedroom you might notice clothes that need to be dry cleaned and an item that needs to be repaired. Sit in front of your computer and mark all of the emails that need to be replied to.

Then think of all the friends that need to be telephoned, and any thank you letters that need to be sent. Also note odd jobs, like putting photos into an album, sewing a button on your blouse, transferring addresses to a new address book, and purchasing items like hooks for the bathroom door, etc. Make a complete list of everything!

I encourage my clients to think BIG! Think of 101 items and write everything on that list. We want this list to be really long. A list of seven things might seem impressive, but it won't include everything so aim to write down 101 things. You might not be able to write everything down in one sitting, and additional items might come to you over a few days.

Go to **www.untappedbrilliance.com/chartsfromthebook** to download a 101 Things Checklist for you to fill out.

Anti-procrastination lists are good because they are a place to download all your tasks and errands that you have been meaning to do, from your mind onto paper. They also give you some focus. When you have some free time often your mind goes blank and you are not sure what to do. If this happens you know you can go to your anti-procrastination list and use your time wisely.

Example of an Anti-Procrastination List

	Item to do	Estimated time	Useful information	Check off when completed
1.	Make dental appointment	5 minutes	Telephone #	
2.	Put holiday photos into albums	60 minutes		

The next step is to go through the list and write the estimated time each task will take, such as the phone call to the dentist may take five minutes. Painting a table might be four hours. Putting down the estimated time the task is likely to take is helpful because first of all, it makes it less scary and second, it helps you decide which tasks you have time for. For example, if you have 15 minutes to spare, you could pick three five-minute tasks or one 15-minute task.

The anti-procrastination list might look a bit scary, but it's there for you to get in control of your life. It's your friend, not your foe.

Project List

Some tasks are made up of lots of different steps. For example, you buy a table from a junk shop which needs to be painted, but then it sits around for months because you never get round to refinishing it. If you break the task down into bite-sized pieces on a project list, it will seem less daunting.

Your project list could look like this:

1. Go to hardware store and buy paint, paint brushes and sand paper.

2. Sand down the table.

3. Paint first coat.

4. Paint second coat.

5. Let dry overnight.

6. Place it in its new home.

Suddenly a task that filled you with dread and seemed so big, now seems manageable, and is something that you will actually do and possibly even enjoy!

Compile a Master List

Take all of the lists that you have now created, and compile a Master List. Check this list when you do your eight-week planning (p. 75 -76). This could be kept in your Untapped Brilliance Binder.

Prioritize Your Master List

Have a look and see what are the most important items on your master list. When deciding which items are a priority, here is an excellent tip: If it affects your health, your reputation, or will cost you money, then it should be classed as a priority. Once those tasks have been eliminated, then you can work on the others. Over the following days and months, you will find that you will be able to work through all the items on the master list.

What Should I Do Today?

When you are considering what you should do on any given day, ask yourself the question, "At the end of the day, what would I feel really good about having accomplished?"

By asking yourself this, you will find you will tackle the important tasks, even if they aren't exactly the most enjoyable ones. For example, phoning the tax office isn't enjoyable. But the unmade call is giving you anxiety, so you will feel really good when you have made the call and got it out of the way.

Time Management

It Is Okay To Say No

People with ADHD often over-commit. When friends suggest an outing or colleagues need a volunteer, your good nature, willingness to help, and impulsivity always has you saying yes. By agreeing to do so many things, you are over-stretched and over-committed. Not only does this mean you don't have time to do things that are really important to you, it also means you will feel frazzled and will often be late.

Delegate

This might not seem an easy action when you live on your own, but there are always people around to help you out. At work, you might be doing something that would be more appropriate for another person to do. At home, you might get a cleaner to help with the housework, an odd jobs person to help with the work you don't like or feel inclined to do, and an accountant to help you with your taxes. Don't feel you have to do something all on your own even if you live on your own.

If something works--keep doing it. It's funny how we forget the things that work for us. It's great when you find a new system that works for you. You read about it, and then get everything you need to implement it, and then put it into practice. Everything is going great until you have to work late one night, or you get the flu. You get off course and then you forget all about the new system, even though it was working for you. Take a few minutes now and try to remember if there was a system or anything that worked for you in the past. If it did, try and implement it again.

Use Your Time Effectively

Doing similar tasks at the same time is a good way to get things done. You might have a batch of telephone calls to make: the dentist, tax office, etc. So sit down with a cup of tea, your list, all the paperwork you need for each call, and start working your way through this list. Once you have made one call, you will find that you experience a 'high'--a feeling of success and of getting a job done, plus relief that you finally did something you have been meaning to do. After the first telephone call, most of the resistance you felt will have evaporated and the other calls will be much easier to make.

Be On Time, Every Time
When you start being on time for your appointments, you will find that your life is actually easier and less stressful. You won't be constantly rushing, and you won't have to think up creative excuses all the time. If you get the reputation of being on time for your appointments, then you also get the reputation of being trustworthy, respectful, and dependable.

Remember than an appointment can be many things: work-related events, family-related events, medical or veterinary appointments, a meeting with friends, hobby-related events, etc. It's better to arrive a little early than a little late for your appointments. You can take things to do so that you don't feel you are wasting your time, for example, bills to pay, birthday cards to write or news to read.

Tips for Arriving On Time (and a few minutes early)
Arriving on time for an appointment does require accurate time estimation. How long does it take you to get up, get dressed, and get out the door in the morning? How long will the drive take? Are there other factors to bear in mind, like bad weather? Will you be traveling in rush hour?

The day before your appointment, have a look at your calendar and see what you have scheduled, then work backwards. If you have an appointment at 9:00 am, what time would you need to leave the house to arrive on time? You need to figure out the amount of time it takes to get ready and then go from point A to point B.

Here's an example of how to calculate your time:
1. 60 minutes in the morning to do your wake up/dressing routine.

2. The drive to your appointment is 30 minutes.

3. Add another 15 minutes due to rush hour traffic.

4. Add an additional 15 minutes to your schedule as it's hard to find parking close to the building.

5. Add another 15 minutes to walk from the parking space to the building where your appointment is.

In this example, in order to make your 9:00 am appointment, you will need to wake up at 6:45 am.

Also apply the backward rule to appointments during the day and evening too. If you are at one location until 2:00 pm, and you need to be at another location for the next meeting at 2:15 pm, but it's a 30-minute drive, there is no possible way you can make your 2:15 appointment on time. Be mindful of this when making appoint-ments. People with ADHD like to do lots of things but you can't be super-human.

Set Concrete Deadlines
Deadlines are great for people with ADHD because you work more productively when you have an end in sight. This means you use your time very wisely. If there isn't a deadline imposed on you by other people, create your own, and then reward yourself when you complete the task.

Find Out What Distracts You

Distractions can be welcome or unwelcome, but either way they stop you from doing what you intended to do. If this is the case with you, then you can formulate a plan to eliminate them. First, identify what distracts you, such as the phone ringing when you are in the middle of a task that requires your attention, watching TV in the morning while getting ready for work and you need to leave the house on schedule, or browsing the internet at a a time when you need to be doing something else. None of these things are bad; it's just all about timing.

Transition Time

Transition between tasks is very difficult for an adult with ADHD because your natural tendencies are to change focus very frequently, or to become hyperfocused on one activity and not want to stop until it is completed.

Here are a few tips to help you make transitions:
- Prepare yourself mentally ahead of time for the activities or tasks that you will be doing.
- Schedule mini-breaks between activities.
- Use your kitchen timer to ensure that you stick to a given task for a specified amount of time before moving to another.
- Plan transition time between activities.
- Work on the least enjoyable tasks first. This is helpful if you hyperfocus, because the enjoyable tasks are hard to stop doing even when you have other important tasks to complete.

Work With Your Body Clock

There are certain times of the day when you are more focused and more energetic. When are your times? Typically, you will have one period in the morning and another one in the evening. So how will you utilize them? Make sure you work with your clock rather than against it. If your productive time is in the morning, use it to do the things that you find the hardest. The weakest times of the day are often after lunch, so use that time to do the things you like to do. Working with your cycles is really helpful and you will notice that you will feel happier and more productive when you do this. If you find your energy flagging, it might be helpful to listen to some really upbeat music, or do a short burst of exercise.

Habits

Habits are a wonderful thing because then the activities that used to occupy so much of your brain now become second nature, and you don't have to keep them spinning around in your conscious mind any more. Good habits are freeing and wonderful things. They allow you to feel accomplished, ahead of the game and happy with yourself. Good news! Even though you have ADHD, you can still develop supportive habits.

Develop Set Routines
Routines are important for someone with ADHD because the more organized you are, the easier life is for you. A routine is a sequence of steps required to perform a certain task. For example your bedtime routine might include a bath, a cup of herbal tea, washing your face, brushing your teeth and taking any medication or vitamins, setting the alarm clock, reading in bed for a few minutes, and then falling asleep. This routine is so ingrained in your life it is now a habit. You don't even think about it. Your body is on autopilot and you can think about other things while going about your normal routine. Just like riding a bike or driving a car, developing routines is very beneficial, as when done often enough they become second nature, and save you a lot of brain work.

What routines could you develop? Give some thought now on what your problem areas may be. What routines would be helpful?

A morning routine to get you up and out the door with everything you need would be very beneficial.

For example, never leave the house without your cell phone, calendar/planner, keys and wallet, and upon returning home always put your keys back on a key hook.

Making a hard copy checklist of your new routine is helpful until you have it safely stored in your long-term memory. You can keep the list in an appropriate place until you have it memorized. For example, stick a 'Don't leave home without' checklist on your main exit door until it's safely ingrained in your memory. A 'Things to do before I leave the office' checklist can be helpful as well. Just work on one routine at a time until it has become second nature and then look at the next routine you would like to develop.

Make a Habit of Preparing For Tomorrow

At some point in the evening, before you go to bed, spend a few minutes with your calendar and master list and plan for the following day. Remind yourself of any appointments you have, gather anything you need for the appointments and place these articles in your bag, then have a look to see what tasks from your master list you would like to do.

This way, in the morning, you are all set to go. You can look at your daily list as a reminder, but you have done all the thinking ahead of time. You don't have to go looking for telephone numbers or paperwork--you are good to go. It takes a little while in the morning for your mind to become awake as your brain is slowly kicking into gear. You have really helped it by doing the thinking, and planning, the day before.

Rewards

Everyone responds well to rewards: children, dogs, and even we adults.

So reward yourself often! The size of the treat will depend on how big the task was. A small task should be rewarded by a small reward while a bigger task is rewarded by a larger reward.

Rewards add an additional incentive to complete the task, and help you to celebrate your success. You don't need to (and shouldn't) save rewards for big tasks. In fact, don't wait to congratulate yourself for finishing your full degree. Reward yourself for every assignment and exam you completed along the way, and for every day you sat and studied hard. Rewards actually get you to work harder in a short period of time.

Rewards are a personal choice. What would be a treat for one person might seem like a punishment to another. Write a list of things that you consider a treat or reward now. Some will be bigger than others, and some will cost money while others won't. For example, taking a bubble bath, phoning a friend, hiking in the country, reading a new book, buying a new album, renting a movie, or enjoying a meal out with a friend are all great rewards.

These are just a few suggestions to get your list started. I often reward myself for going to the gym with a quick browse in the nearby bookstore. Going to the grocery store can be a drag, but it seems much more enticing if I promise myself time to look through a magazine while I am there.

ACTIONS

1. Buy and use a calendar! For help on selecting the best calendar for your ADHD brain, go to **www.untappedbrilliance.com/yourcalendar**

2. Compile a Master List including:
   --Anti-procrastination List
   --Decluttering List (see Step 6)
   You can find charts for this and other actions in this chapter in the Charts section at the back of this book. Or, to get printable charts go to
   www.untappedbrilliance.com/chartsfromthebook

3. Start using a daily 'to do' list.

4. Commit to arriving to two of your appointments this week a few minutes early.

5. Create routines for yourself to take the brainwork out of life's basic tasks.

6. Join me for my free annual planning challenge! Go to **www.untappedbrilliance.com/planyouryear** to get on the next participant invite list.

STEP NINE

Boost Your Self-Esteem

"Nothing builds self-esteem and self-confidence like accomplishment"
—Thomas Carlyle

Our self-esteem is related to how we feel and view ourselves. If we feel good about ourselves, then we have a higher self-esteem than if we feel bad about ourselves. This self-awareness is part of being human. We have an identity and we decide if we like it or not. Unfortunately as humans, we are naturally very critical of ourselves. Our inner voice can be very mean and critical, which can be destructive and painful.

Reasons for Low Self-esteem in People With ADHD

Self-esteem levels are often low in adults with ADHD, after years of not measuring up to society's 'norms.' You probably had many negative messages given to you from the outside world on a daily basis. In addition, ADHD is often linked with learning disabilities such as dyslexia, so you might have been labeled or felt 'not that bright.'

Social skills can also be problematic for ADHD children. Receiving a lot of negative feedback, not doing well academically and/or socially, are three key ways self-esteem can suffer. It is unfortunate this happens, as these are your formative years where your mind is developing and being shaped. If you hear negative messages externally, then you repeat the negative messages internally too. As an adult with ADHD, your self-esteem could still be suffering. If you compare yourself to others, the everyday tasks that seem effortless to them can be very problematic to you, making you feel worthless.

Low self-esteem can result in:

Anxiety	Procrastination
Stress	Blaming others
Loneliness	Breaking rules
Depression	Fighting authority
Problems in relationships	Difficulty coping in the world
Problems in friendships	Lack of responsibility
Impaired academic and job performance	Lack of assertiveness
Underachievement	Body image problems
Drug and alcohol abuse	Poor quality of life
Perfectionism	Negative self-talk

Benefits of Healthy Self-esteem

The good news is, once you realize your self-esteem is low, you can start doing lots of things to change it. Healthy self-esteem is something that can be achieved at any time or any age.

Having healthy self-esteem is being able to gauge ourselves

accurately and be able to acknowledge and appreciate ourselves unconditionally. This means being able to recognize your strengths and weaknesses realistically and acknowledge yourself as valuable and significant without conditions or doubts. You know you are still a good person even if you had an argument with a co-worker, or made a mistake.

Some people with ADHD are concerned that they will become arrogant or boastful if they have healthy or high self-esteem. But that won't happen! Those are not characteristics of someone with healthy self-esteem. If you see them, it is usually in someone with low self-esteem trying to appear confident. When you have good self-esteem, you have an inner confidence and self-assurance, so you don't need to brag.

When you feel good about yourself, you know and believe in your abilities. With this type of attitude, you *can* achieve and do anything. The good news is, all the steps in the Untapped Brilliance System will help increase your self-esteem.

Benefits of increasing your self-esteem are:

1. Increased confidence.
2. Happiness.
3. Increased respect of yourself.
4. Increased respect of others.
5. Increased achievements in *all* areas of life.
6. Feeling that you are flying high.
7. Ability to roll with the punches.

Ways to Increase Your Self-Esteem

Inner Voice
Your inner voice is a powerful part of self-esteem. If yours is critical of you and your achievements and constantly telling you negative messages, then you will have low self-esteem. We want yours to be positive, encouraging, reassuring, and congratulatory.

The inner critic can make you feel bad about everything you say or do and stop you from reaching your goals. Without a doubt you are your own worst critic. The things you say to yourself are things you would never say to anyone else as they can be rude, mean and negative.

Start to pay attention to what your inner voice is saying. It would be impossible to know everything it says, as our inner voice is constantly chatting away. Some messages are very fleeting while others stay in the conscious mind long enough for you to be aware of what they are, and these are the ones you will be able to write down.

The chatter, good or bad, that takes place in our minds directly affects our bodies. This lesson was demonstrated to me one hot summer Sunday morning while running with my run-club friends.

Usually, I can run at a good speed, but this Sunday it was a real struggle. I was frustrated with myself because it was hard going. My legs felt heavy, my lungs couldn't get enough air, and I was falling behind the rest of the group. Then I heard the message from my inner voice saying, "You shouldn't have stayed out so late last night! No wonder you are finding it hard as you didn't go for a run this past week! These girls are much younger than you, and you are getting old." When I realized what I was hearing, I decided to tell myself something different and simply said instead "You are doing really well, you are doing really well!" In a matter of seconds (no exaggeration here!) I noticed my speed began to pick up. In a few minutes I went from being one of the runners at the back, to being one of those in front. I kept up this simple mantra and the rest of the run became pleasurable. Think about what tapes play in your head and what you could say instead. You might not be a runner, but the messages you say to yourself do seriously affect your performance in the world. Your voice can only tell you one message at a time, so keep the messages positive ones.

Not All Inner Voices Are Bad

Don't do something that you feel you should do, when something inside of you is telling you a different message. Some people call this their intuition or 'listening to their gut.' When you listen to your body, you will do things that feel right for you, and you will feel happier. This can be applied to small choices, such as if to have chicken or fish for dinner, or to bigger decisions like when to change jobs. When you follow your heart, your actions are inspired by you, and the actions are easier to carry out because they feel right. The payoff is that you will be much happier. When you listen to yourself, you build up self-reliance and trust in yourself. This is all part of having high and healthy self-esteem.

Counteract the Negative Message With a Positive One

When you hear yourself talking in a negative way, take a moment to counter the message in a reasonable voice with a positive message. For example, if you are on the computer and something happens that you didn't want to happen, you might say "I am so stupid" or "I have messed up yet again." Respond by telling yourself, "No, I am not stupid and I can figure this out!" Or if you hear, "Did you really mess it up again?" simply reply, "No, you just pressed the wrong button by mistake." Your negative voice is very dramatic and makes lots of sweeping generalizations, but it doesn't like the voice of reason, and when your reasonable voice kicks in, it is like pouring water on fire.

With negative messages you find yourself saying over and over, have a countering positive one ready to respond to it. For example, if your inner voice says "I am so _____" counter it with something like "Actually, I am pretty smart" or "Actually, there are things I am good at." Next, think of a fact from your life to support this new positive message. Perhaps, "I passed my driver's exam the first time" or "I am good in an emergency."

The words we use are important as they really affect our thoughts and views about ourselves. Negative words can make us feel bad about ourselves and lower our energy and mood. The word 'should' is a good example, as in, "I should be able to do this" or "I should have a partner/be married" or "I should own my own house by now." When 'should' appears in our thoughts we can feel guilt or shame or annoyance that we haven't met our high standards. However, we can remove 'should' and rephrase the sentence to "I can figure this out," "I would like to get married one day," or "I will own my own house when the time is right." It then becomes a comforting or empowering thought.

Self-nurturing

In order to have good self-esteem, it is important to take care of yourself physically. Essential self-care is personal hygiene, bathing, washing and styling your hair, brushing your teeth, keeping your nails cut and clean, washing your clothes, cooking healthy food, living in a tidy and clean place and getting enough sleep and exercise. The list could also include going to the dentist, getting your hair cut regularly, having an annual check-up with your doctor, getting your eyes tested and other such basics.

Keep your home in the condition it looks like when you have guests coming, even if you are not expecting anyone. You deserve it and, again, it feeds your subconscious the message that you are just as worthy as anyone else, not less worthy.

Eat good, healthy food. Take the time to shop, cook and eat regular meals even if you are on your own. Check out the Nourish Yourself chapter for more instruction on this.

Take time to have fun and relax; you deserve it. If you need tips on having fun, go to Step 11. When we feel bad about ourselves, we don't feel we deserve to do fun things, but this is when we actually need to have more fun!

Exercise is a great way to boost self-esteem because you are taking care of yourself both in the present moment and for the future. It increases confidence, happiness and a sense of self-reliance, and improves your self-image.

Appreciate Your Genes

Today's society places a high emphasis on what we look like, and we have unrealistic standards if we compare ourselves to the airbrushed pictures of models, actors and actresses we see in magazines and online.

We are all born with our own body type, and it's helpful to enjoy and work with what we have. Some things you can change, some things you can't. You can develop six-pack abs, but you can't grow six inches. Look at your body and decide if there is something you could do to make yourself feel better about your body.

For example, if you'd feel more energetic or your blood work would be healthier, then losing five to 15 pounds could be a realistic goal. Now you're ready to do something about it. You could join Weight Watchers, use the Noom app, or take another proactive approach.

People with low self-esteem can be critical of their body image, and think that if they change that aspect of themselves, then everything else in their life will be perfect. Remember that in terms of looks, when beautiful models or actors and actresses are interviewed, they were often bullied or laughed at in their past for physical traits that most people now prize and consider beautiful.

Fake It Until You Make It

Even if you don't feel like taking the time to look good when you leave the house, always make the effort. The better you look on the outside, the better you feel on the inside. It's a 'chicken and egg' situation. Wear your good clothes, spray on some aftershave or perfume, and by making that extra effort, you will be repaid by how much better you feel on the inside. You might get some compliments, or catch your reflection and be pleasantly surprised, all of which give your morale a boost.

Also, wear nice clothes in your home as well, even if no one else will see you, because we want you to feel good about yourself all the time, not just when you are going out. If you wear your dirty sweatpants all the time, it is sending negative messages to your subconscious. Make a rule to dress only in clothes that make you feel great and ditch the old ones.

Celebrate and Acknowledge Your Accomplishments

People with ADHD aren't usually very good at acknowledging their own accomplishments. They feel that they have happened by 'fluke' or that they would not be able to duplicate them again. They often feel like a fake, and they are tricking the rest of the world with a facade that might disappear at any moment.

However, it is important to acknowledge your own achievements and take credit for them. You achieved them--no one else. When you acknowledge what you have achieved in your life so far, it helps to make you feel good about yourself and helps increase your self-esteem. If you accomplish something or achieve something great, it is important that you acknowledge it. You can celebrate with friends or mark the event by doing something good for yourself, but the important thing is that it doesn't go unnoticed by you.

Success Journal

Create a 'success journal' portion in your Untapped Brilliance Binder. This is where you document all the things you do that you are proud of. For example, if you worked hard to get a report done on time, completed your taxes, or overcame procrastination and got something done, write it in your binder. Anything that you did that you felt good about accomplishing should be noted there.

Also in the success journal, document positive feedback from others, such as getting a compliment on your hair, your performance, someone saying how much they like your sense of humor or another personal quality. Write it all down. This will be a positive reinforcement of you and all your great achievements. When you are low, it's hard to remember these events and comments. That is why it's important to document them, so you can refer to them at any time, particularly when you are feeling low.

Create a brag folder where you can keep all your certificates, awards, references, thank you notes for great work, etc. Better yet, frame your qualifications and put them on the wall somewhere in your home and create a wall of fame for yourself.

Other People

Positive people in your life can be a big help to build up your self-esteem. It can be tricky for someone with low self-esteem to ask others for help, but be brave and ask, because the payoff will be very beneficial.

Ask your closest friends to tell you what it is they like about you, and ask your loved ones why they love you. Keep these comments in your 'Success Journal' and remind yourself of them often. This is a valuable step because then you will have a clear insight into how the world views you, compared to the distorted view that you may have.

Also, when you start to give people in your life compliments, you will notice they start to do the same in return. When you are generous with your sincere compliments, they will be returned to you. For example, if you are talking to a friend and you realize that she is always a really good listener, or fun company, tell her. If someone has had their hair done and it suits them, tell them. The more freely you give compliments, the more they will be returned.

Part of self-esteem is related to how people have treated us, both in the past and also how they treat us now. If you haven't been treated well, then it is quite likely your self-esteem will be low. It is particularly important that you start treating yourself well immediately. When you start doing this, others will follow suit. If you have low self-esteem, there is a high chance you are a people pleaser, and constantly put other peoples' needs before your own. Even if you are part of a couple and have children, you sometimes ought to put your needs first. When you are happy and fulfilled, you are in a much stronger place to be a good partner or parent. It is not possible to run on empty and still keep on giving.

Try not to compare yourself to others, as this can make you feel inferior and further decrease your self-esteem. If someone has something you would like, whether it is a personality trait, accomplishments, something they own, or a lifestyle they have, use it to inspire you. Don't compare yourself with others and feel you aren't doing as well. Be grateful to them for helping you to identify something you would like. Remember that anything is possible. You are unique. There is only one person in this world that has your gifts and talents, and that is you!

Proactive Ways to Increase Your Self-Esteem

Plan an Adventure
Plan a trip or an activity you have never tried before. When you stretch your comfort boundaries, you also increase your self-esteem.

Take Stock of Your Life
What is working in your life and what isn't? Of the things that aren't working brainstorm what you could do to change them. Make an action plan.

Think about and write down at least five occasions when you were doing something that you didn't think you would be able to accomplish, but you did anyway. Think about and write down the times when you knew that you could do something, even when no one else believed you could.

Think about and write down your twenty biggest accomplishments that you are most proud of. Perhaps getting a degree or certification, raising your children, running a race, or moving to a different part of the country. Think about how you felt when you finished something that was a challenge for you.

What are you really good at? What do you excel at? Do more of these things. There is no greater way to boost your self-esteem than to perform the things that you are naturally good at.

Learn something new, anything that stretches you and takes you out of your comfort zone. It will make you feel proud of yourself.

Write a list of things you would like to change. Maybe it is to get to a healthy weight, change jobs, etc. When you start to take action towards making changes in your life by taking control, you also start to feel better about yourself.

If you feel your self-esteem is very debilitating, find a good therapist and start working together on this issue. They have professional training in helping you with your self-esteem.

Think About Getting a Dog

Dogs are a great way to boost your self-esteem. They are completely non-judgmental and provide you with unconditional love regardless of whether you remembered to take the trash out or didn't do well at work that day. They are always incredibly happy to see you even if you were gone for only a few minutes. They force you to go for walks, so you will never forget your daily exercise. They provide you with structure to your day. They need you to wake up in the morning at a fairly regular time so they can go for a walk. And since you know you are going to have to wake up at roughly the same times every morning, this also forces you to go to bed at a sensible time every night.

Dog owners talk to lots more people when they are out and about because people approach you and engage you in conversation. So it's a great way to have social interaction. In his book *The Real Age Makeover* Dr. Roizen says that pet owners do not suffer as many bouts of depression and maintain better self-esteem. Dogs are warm beings that love to be hugged. If you live on your own, it's great to have the physical contact.

Join Toastmasters

Since most people would rather die than speak in public, learning this skill is a great way to build your confidence and self-esteem. This is a skill that positively affects all aspects of your life. By learning how to speak in public, it will be easier to speak to a stranger, make a phone call, look someone in the eye when you are in a conversation with them, and talk in front of small groups of people at work or at parties. It also aids in your assertiveness and helps you ask for what you want from loved ones and strangers.

The confidence that this skill gives you spills over into all other areas of your life and you begin to shine. If you can speak in front of a group of strangers, then you can speak to anyone. Not many people in this world have this skill and you will have a talent that few possess.

The best way to learn to speak in public is to join a group such as Toastmasters. Another good reason to join is you will meet some new positive people. To find the group nearest to you, you can do a search online at www.toastmasters.org.

ACTIONS

1. Create a Success Journal! There is a chart for starting this at the back of the book. You can get a printable chart from **www.untappedbrilliance.com/chartsfromthebook**

2. Record all your success and compliments in your Success Journal.

3. Create a brag folder or wall of fame.

4. Counteract negative messages with positive ones.

5. Practice self-nurturing.

6. Work through the proactive exercises to increase your self-esteem.

7. Celebrate your successes!

STEP TEN

Create a Group of Wonderful People in Your Life

"A friend is someone who lets you have total freedom to be yourself"
— **Jim Morrison**

In order to lead a healthy, well-balanced life, it is important to have some special people in your life so you feel connected, loved, cared for and valued. Humans, including those with ADHD, are social beings, and we need human connection to thrive. Making time for people can seem like a luxury when in fact it is essential.

Some people with ADHD do very well in social settings; they have highly developed social skills and love interacting with people. Other people with ADHD do not do well in social situations and find them very difficult.

Social skills are key components to building a happy life. We need these skills to succeed in life, just as we need food and shelter. Not being able to relate to people can cause problems with self-esteem, unhappiness and lost career opportunities and result in feeling isolated and depressed.

If you are a person who finds it hard to meet new people and develop new friendships, then you don't necessarily need to become a social butterfly. But human connection adds meaning to life and it's an important key to fulfilling your potential.

Positive Human Contact Is Vital

People with ADHD often get a lot of negative feedback from others, so it's important to counteract that with lots of positive comments as well. When you share your life with even a few close friends it reduces stress and eases discouragement.

Hang Out With People Who Love You Warts and All

Be sure to hang out with people who see your strengths, your great personality, your energy, and your humor and don't see your weaknesses as problems. For example, some people are very particular about time-keeping and if you arrive a few minutes late they are negative and grumpy with you for the rest of the time together. If time-keeping is not one of your strengths (although hopefully it will improve with the suggestions in this book), those people are not your best type of friends. Good people for you are the types that keep themselves busy until you arrive and then are delighted to see you when you appear and enjoy spending time with you. Those lost few minutes really don't matter to them.

One of my clients is very energetic. She has a hard time sitting still and she tells stories with her arms waving in the air for emphasis. This is a trait that makes her who she is and her friends love being with her and enjoy her energy, including her extravagant gestures. When she started to date a very conservative man he was embarrassed and irritated by these movements, particularly when they were out with his friends or family. It became increasingly difficult for my client to conform to his wishes and she was becoming distressed, sad, and losing confidence trying to be someone she was not. The moral of this story is to be with people who love you for who you are, not for who you could be if you changed your ways to suit them. Changing for others can make your self-esteem plummet. It can also lead to depression.

It's very important to learn how to check in with yourself, and ask, "Does this feel right to me?" If not, stop the situation straight away. It can be very hard to do, and that's why it's important to surround yourself with understanding and kind people.

Having people in your life involves choices and effort. When you are leading a busy life, or fighting to keep on top of things, time spent chatting with friends seems like a luxury that you can cut out. However, don't do it! To lead a well-balanced, healthy life it's important to make time to do small things that bring you pleasure. Making a new friend takes time, as you need to get to know them and trust them. The best way to have good friends is to be a good friend.

Family

Most people consider these people their core people--the people they spend the most time with and love the most. These people are both your immediate family unit and your extended family. However, some people feel very different about their family; they may not be in touch with them. If this is the case, then it is important that you have a 'chosen' family made up of very close friends.

If you don't live near your family, technology makes it fairly easy to keep in touch. Telephone, video calls, and group chats are a few options. This way, you can show you care, and feel cared for.

Friends

Good friends become like extended family, and very often you spend more time with these people than your second cousin twice removed. With your friends you often have a lot in common and enjoy the same types of activities. There is the saying that we don't choose our family, but we can choose our friends. This is very true, so make sure you choose really good ones!

Co-workers

These people are a big part of your life because you see them every day. It is important that you work in a positive environment. If you don't, it can affect you negatively and then it might be time to move to another job.

Community

Even if you live in a big city you are still likely to shop at the same stores, go to the same dry cleaners, the gym, the same gas station, etc. These people become part of your community. If you go to activities and clubs, or volunteer, these people are also part of your community.

Service Providers

Search for good service providers such as dentists, opticians, doctors, chiropractors, massage therapists, hairdressers, etc., until you find ones that you feel comfortable and at ease with. Try a few until you bond with someone. These people are not your best friends, but you will be dealing with them on a regular basis, and these are people who you have a choice about letting into your life. When you find someone good, keep going. You will form a professional bond that lets you feel supported and taken care of.

Reconnecting With Old Friends

There might have been people in your past that you liked and enjoyed the company of, but you lost touch with them for some reason. When thinking about building up your network of friends, it might be worth trying to reconnect with some old friends too. The internet has now made this really easy. The most obvious websites for this are www.linkedin.com and www.facebook.com where many people are reconnecting with friends from the past, as well as meeting new ones. You may find your old friends on apps like Instagram also. LinkedIn is primarily used for professional work and business purposes, but once someone accepts your connection invite, you can message them and go from there if you are both interested in more interaction.

Where Could You Meet New Friends?

If you would like to broaden your network of friends, you could join a club centered on a topic or activity that you are interested in, such as a hiking or running club. Or you could learn a new skill such as cooking, take martial arts classes, go to a meditation class or take an art or photography class. The benefit of joining a club or group is that you are with people that you have a natural bond with straight away as you both share a similar interest. Toastmasters is another great way to make friends.

www.meetup.com hosts a lot of information about many clubs and groups in your local area. If you are at one of these clubs and you think someone might be interested in getting to know you on a deeper level, then make the first move and invite the person to join you for a coffee. That first move will show you like them and are interested in getting to know them at a deeper level than just club members. This can move the friendship forward.

The Untapped Brilliance Club

I created The Untapped Brilliance Club for positive, proactive people living with ADHD. It's a great way to make friends and be part of a ready-made supportive community. Also, being with people who understand you (because they are very similar) helps build your confidence. You can find more information about the Club on the last page of this book.

Keeping in Touch With Your Friends

Keeping in touch with friends you already have can be tricky. You might 'sort of forget' about them, then when you remember, feel bad that it's been a while and procrastinate making contact. Or, you might talk yourself out of making a phone call because you worry you'd be intruding on them. Try not to overthink it; instead, send a quick message with a text or a voice message when you think of a friend.

With friends that live near you, you might set up a regular meeting, like brunch on the last Saturday of every month. While you are actually with friends, get out your calendar and plan the next time you will meet. Even if it's not for three months, at least you will have something booked. The time will pass by very quickly!

ADHDers often like to do things on the spur of the moment, which is great and often works out well. However, if most people in your life are planners, you might find yourself suggesting a get-together that evening only to find out they have had an existing plan for a while. If this is the case for you, try to plan a little ahead yourself, so you'll see more of your friends.

Be There For Your Friends

One of the best ways to have good friends in your life is to be a good friend. Doing thoughtful things for people is greatly appreciated. Birthday cards are the perfect reason to send your friend something through the mail or to phone them and wish them a great day. Remembering someone's special day is really meaningful and it shows you care.

If a friend is facing a stressful situation in their life, you can be there for them for that, either by listening to them or doing an act of kindness. This helps to deepen the friendship further.

Friendships Are Equal

It is important that your friendships are equal. People with ADHD can be too nice, and give and give and make lots of compromises to keep the friendship ticking along. However, be careful of this. There should be equal amounts of give and take in your friendships. Of course, if a friend is in a crisis, then you will give more of yourself during that time, but they should be there for you during a crisis of your own. Also, pay attention to make sure you aren't the one giving all your time. People with ADHD are usually givers or takers. You want to strive for middle ground.

Because people with ADHD often have low self-esteem, they often don't expect a great deal from the people they hang out with. Hopefully, this book will be the spark that makes you realize that you deserve to be treated well, and will raise the standards for the people you allow into your life. Think of what you ideally would like in a friendship and strive to get it.

Keep Your Word

If you say you are going to be somewhere, or will do something for someone, then it is vital that you do what you say. If you do not, your friends will stop trusting you, and since trust is the key to a successful relationship, you want to avoid this happening.

You might forget what you said you would do, or you might over-commit and say you will do too much and be unable to follow through. Your calendar will help you with these issues. It is better to say 'no' to something than to say 'yes' and let someone down.

Communicating With People

Often people with ADHD have problems relating to people, which may have its roots in childhood. Let's look at some common problems and some possible solutions.

A Two-Way Process
Communication is a two-way process and you want your companion to feel heard and feel special. Try to make eye contact with the person you are talking to without staring.

Staying on Subject
If someone is talking about one subject, try to stay on that subject before jumping to the next one. A distraction might mean you didn't pay attention to what is being said. If you find your mind wandering off, try to keep involved with what is going on around you. You might ask the speaker a few questions, or paraphrase what they said back to them, just to stay on track.

The Importance of Listening
Interrupting when the other person is speaking can be perceived as you being not interested in what the other person has to say. If you really want to say something and it accidentally just pops out of your

mouth, simply say, "I am sorry I interrupted. Please carry on."

Think Before Speaking
Voicing your opinion without first thinking how it could be perceived by the other person can be considered rude. If you sense they were hurt or offended, a simple apology will usually smooth things over. But you should strive to consider people's feelings before making the potentially rude comment.

Allow the Conversation to Flow
Don't feel you are responsible for keeping the entire conversation running smoothly. Gaps of silence are a normal part of any conversation. Feeling the responsibility to keep the conversation going can be very tiring. The other person might simply need a few seconds to gather their thoughts before they begin their next sentence.

Recognize Non-verbal Clues
Learn to read non-verbal communication signs. You could get a book or watch videos on the subject, so you can understand the non-verbal communications you are giving to others, as well as the same style of communication signals they are sending to you. For example, if someone looks at their watch, or is heading towards the door, then it means they are ready to leave and it's your cue to wind down the conversation. Also, pay attention to the tone of their voice.

If you would like more ideas on communication, there are many books on the market, including *How to Win Friends and Influence People*. In this book, Dale Carnegie gives many great tips on communicating with people. It is definitely worth reading.

Listen to Your Body
After being with a group of people, ask yourself, "Do I feel happier,

or depleted?" If the answer is 'depleted,' then it would be good to limit your time with these people, or question what it is about them that makes you feel like this. If you meet someone and you realize they aren't making you feel good about yourself, or you feel uneasy in their company, then it's time to move on. For every one of these people, there will be another person who makes you feel clever, amazing and funny. When you keep the 'not quite good' people in your life, there is no room to meet the great people. Learn to pass up the no-so-good for the 'great.'

When you are selective like this, it may mean that you'll spend a few evenings alone when you would have preferred to go out and do something fun. However, it's in this time that you will be able to reflect and become inspired to think how to meet new people. Your options are limitless.

Don't assume people do things intentionally to upset you. Often it's just a mistake. After a lifetime of hearing people saying mean things, often people with ADHD become overly sensitive to others' behavior, which may not have been intended to be negative. For example, if someone pushed ahead of you while you're waiting in line at the store, you can get really upset, or you can say, "Excuse me, you might not realize that the line starts here" and point to the line behind you.

People with ADHD often live outside of themselves and don't pay attention to what is going on inside and their personal needs. It is important to get in touch with what is going on inside you, and to know what makes you happy. When you have a good understanding of what makes you tick, then you are in a better place to convey that to others. You might feel that you are constantly letting people down because of your ADHD, and so you don't feel you deserve to pay attention to yourself, but you really do. It is only when you are able to make yourself happy that you can go on to making those around you happy too.

ACTIONS

1. Are there any people in your life at the moment that put you down or make you feel bad about yourself? If there are, it might be wise to spend less time with these people, or even let the friendship fizzle out. It's much better to spend time with great people.

2. If you are surrounded by negative co-workers, and it is an unpleasant atmosphere, seriously consider getting a new job. It might sound dramatic, but daily stress like this takes a long-term toll on your health as well as on your daily mental psyche.

3. If you have a truly great friend who says or does things that upset you, you can speak up. In a kind and loving way tell them that you really appreciate them in your life, but when they do _____, it hurts you.

4. Consider joining a club that interests you and meet people who have similar interests to you. Try www.meetup.com.

5. Pay attention to your own needs and feelings.

6. Read *How to Win Friends and Influence People* by Dale Carnegie. (Don't be put off by the title!)

7. Sign up to linkedin.com or facebook.com if you are interested in reconnecting with old friends you have lost touch with.

8. To learn tips on how to use Facebook to keep in touch with friends (even if social media usually feels overwhelming), read this article on the Untapped Brilliance Blog www.untappedbrilliance.com/adhd-adults-2/

STEP ELEVEN

Have Fun!

"Fun is about as good a habit as there is."

— Unknown

Life is supposed to be fun, and yet so often it isn't.

Many people with ADHD are stressed, overwhelmed and depressed. So I thought it was important to include a chapter on fun because life really is supposed to be fun, rather than something to be endured. You can start having fun this minute. It does not have to be a delayed reward for when your house is in order, or you have achieved another benchmark in your life. There will always be stresses and strains in your life, so take the bull by the horns and make the decision now to start to have fun!

When I first moved from England to Canada, I was asked this question by a new friend, "So... what do you do for fun?" It was the first time anyone had ever asked me that and I was in my late 20's at the time. Since then I have been asked that question many times, and it has become easier and easier to answer. I no longer have to search around the dusty corners of my brain to think of something to say.

I am going to turn the tables and ask you that question now. So what do you do for fun? **Here are some examples of activities that some people find fun to do:**

1. Hobbies.

2. Volunteer activities (only if you find it actually enjoyable, not something that you feel obligated to do).

3. Relaxing.

4. Something sports-related or physical exercise.

5. Cultural activities.

6. Creative endeavors.

7. Fun for just the sake of having fun!

Take time to think right now about all the things you love to do. This exercise is often hard for some people, so really put your thinking cap on to do this. If you aren't sure if you are already doing things in your life that you find fun, then check in with yourself and ask, "Am I having fun doing this?" For example, if you are in a book store browsing through bookshelves ask, "Am I enjoying myself?"

Having fun can encompass many things. What is fun for you? What do you enjoy doing the most? Is it something active? A sport, perhaps, or exercise? Is it something creative, such as painting, scrapbooking, or restoring furniture?

Is it cultural? Do you love art museums and foreign movies? Perhaps you love cooking, spending time with people or just spending time with yourself. If you are not sure what you find fun, try some new things. Take a dance class, even if you have two left feet, or a cooking class if your idea of cooking is merely opening a can of soup. The great thing about fun is that it has a snowball effect. While you might feel that taking time out to have fun is trivial, in fact the more fun you have, the more the routine and 'boring stuff' will become easier for you to do.

So take time to have fun. Mix it up too! Just as it's not good to eat the same foods every day, we should also try many different things in the fun department.

What Is Fun for You?

Some people become so focused on the hard things in life that they forget what is fun, enjoyable and joyful to them. My clients feel guilty about having fun because they feel there is so much they should be doing instead to catch up, like paying bills, tidying, etc. As you have have been following the steps of the "Brilliance System,"eating good food, exercising, decluttering, and more, having fun is just as essential a step as the more 'serious' steps. So do not skip this part: it's time to schedule some fun! If your type of fun is different from other peoples', and even if someone else thinks your idea of fun is weird or nerdy, or just plain boring, that's OK, because it is fun for you.

Although it might be fun to drink, smoke, or overeat, these acttivities have negative side-effects. It is possible to have lots of fun without substances that alter our minds or bodies.

Become a Weekend Warrior!

Some clients with ADHD say that during the week things are fine. They have a routine: they go to work, exercise, go to after-work activities, come home, eat, watch their favorite shows, and go to bed. They are productive, focused, and happy. But then the weekend comes, the time they are 'supposed' to feel happy and relaxed, and yet they feel depressed, lethargic, bored, unproductive, and unmotivated. They sleep for long periods, feel restless, and are generally miserable until Monday rolls around again.

Weekends for most people are a wonderful two days of unstructured play and relaxation time. But if you have ADHD, then these days can be anything but fun. The reasons are many, but basically, you like having goals, activities, and stimulation. While relaxing is important, it's not really fun for you like it is for others.

If this is true for you, then set a routine in place for yourself for the weekends as well. Perhaps schedule an 11:00 am brunch with friends on Saturday morning, an early morning Sunday run, a regular night out on Saturday evening or a low-key movie night on Sunday evening. You might also set up other routines and rituals for yourself, like drinking your morning coffee in bed on Saturday mornings with a magazine, or taking your dog for a really long walk on Sunday morning.

This type of semi-structured weekend plan allows for time to be spent with people, to get that stimulation and inspiration. It also allows for some down time to catch up on errands or household chores in between.

Make Themes and Fun Goals!

If you enjoy watching a movie on a Sunday evening do not leave finding a good one to chance. Instead of scrolling through Netflix trying to find something that grabs your attention, plan ahead and have themes. For example, 'Oscar-nominated films released in 2005' or Audrey Hepburn films. Having themes for a month or so will help you make your selections easier.

Fun goals give you some direction; they allow you to have some variety and structure at the same time. My Dad is great at creating themes and fun goals. For example, during the Wimbledon Championship, his goal was to eat strawberries every day, which reflects the English tradition of having strawberries and cream with afternoon tea while watching tennis. He likes to collect stamps, but rather than randomly collecting them, he has themes, such as 'all English Christmas stamps.' This embraces his interest and gives him a focus.

It is important to plan and motivate yourself to have fun, just as it important to plan and motivate yourself for work-related goals. One of my clients loves to read, so he has a goal of reading one book a week. This isn't to pressure himself. Rather, it is to encourage him to do what he loves doing, but in a way that makes him feel like he is achieving something, too.

Live Life to the Max!

We are only on this planet once so let's make every second count! Every day, every second can be miserable and boring, or it can be rewarding and fun. Trying new and different things creates new memories. Every time you do something out of your comfort zone it's a stretch, but it soon becomes your new 'norm' and your world becomes bigger.

Learning how to use new technology, visiting a new art show, listening to a different type of music, filling your life with new and different experiences, learning new information, or traveling all add up to a stimulating and fun life.

Create Wonderful Memories!

In her book *The Best Year of Your Life*, Debbie Ford suggests that you create a 'memory day' every month for yourself and your family or friends. These days are so special and out of the ordinary that you will remember them forever. They don't need to cost a lot of money, but they are fun and special. One example she mentions is a day where the whole family watches movies and eats popcorn. What special things could you do to create memories?

Do Something Fun With Important People in Your Life!

For example, mom and daughter 'shop till you drop' trips that include stopping at coffee shops for pit stops. My brother, his wife and I have a tradition on New Year's Day, where we go for a long afternoon walk and then watch Agatha Christie movies.

Seasons come and go quite fast, particularly summer, as we all look forward to it so much. Embrace each season. At the start of each season--summer, fall, winter, and spring--write a list of all the things you would like to do to embrace each of them. Some things might be quite standard, as in winter putting up a Christmas tree or building a snowman (if you live in the Northern hemisphere!)

Other things might be very personal to you, but nonetheless these are important symbols of the season. Eating breakfast outside in the summer could be one example of something you love about summer.

Here is a list of suggestions of fun things to do for every season:

Winter
1. Wrap your Christmas presents while listening to Christmas carols.
2. Decorate your home with holiday decorations.
3. Watch *It's a Wonderful Life*.
4. Build a snowman.
5. Go skiing.
6. Go for a walk and then drink hot chocolate with marshmallows.
7. Make heart-shaped cookies for Valentine's Day.

Spring
1. Watch the St. Patrick's Day Parade.
2. Paint Easter eggs.
3. Play an April Fool's joke.
4. Eat a hot cross bun.

Summer
1. Go for a bike ride.
2. Eat breakfast outside.
3. Eat ice cream.
4. Read an awesome novel.
5. Wear flip-flops.

Fall
1. Sign up for a class and participate in a back-to-school activity.
2. Carve out a pumpkin for Halloween.
3. Drink apple cider.
4. Celebrate Thanksgiving.

If money is a concern, then set aside a certain amount of it in your budget marked specifically for your 'fun' activities. Remember: fun does not have to be expensive. In fact, it is often free, or a minimal expenditure.

Something that brings me joy is a big pot that I plant flowers in every summer. I water and prune the flowers and enjoy watching them blossom and grow. My cat is the fluffiest cat you'll ever meet. She has endless energy and an inquisitive nature and makes me laugh aloud at least once a day.

Check out the newspaper for things that pique your interest. Often some of them are free. Share a funny story from your day with your partner or friend. It may be a conversation you had, or something that you saw. When you start to look for funny things or moments to share with someone, there are suddenly lots of them around.

As an adult with ADHD, there is a high chance that you are a fun person. Fun people are not just the loud, boisterous, slapstick humor Jim Carey types; fun people come in all packages and are a joy to be around. They have an easy smile, a great sense of humor, and make even the most ordinary tasks enjoyable.

While you are doing all these fun activities, there is a good chance you are laughing, too. Laughter is said to be the best medicine, because it does all of the following!

1. Reduces stress and stress-related diseases such as high blood pressure, ulcers, and strokes.
2. Elevates your mood.
3. Enhances your immune system.
4. Improves brain functioning.
5. On-the-spot relaxation technique.
6. Humor can turn a bad situation into a funny one.
7. Unites you with both strangers and loved ones.

ACTIONS

1. What is fun for you?
   There are charts at the back of this book to help you figure this out! You can also download printable charts from **www.untappedbrilliance.com/chartsfromthebook**

2. Think of how you can create themes or goals around what is fun for you.

3. What new things would you like to try?

4. What memory days could you create?

5. Who are the people in your life you most like to do fun things with?

6. Embrace each season.

7. Remember to laugh when you are having fun -- it's good for you!

8. For more information and inspiration about having fun when you have ADHD check out this popular article on The Untapped Brilliance Blog: **www.untappedbrilliance.com/adhd-and-fun**

Congratulations!

You reached the end of the book! Reading is challenging for many people with ADHD, so this in itself is an achievement. Again, congratulations.

If you are reading this page, it also means you have been implementing the 11 steps of the Untapped Brilliance System into your life. High fives! You'll have started to notice their benefits on you and your ADHD and you might even have begun to forget what your old normal was like.

A quick word of warning. In times of stress or change, perhaps an illness, moving house, or a vacation, you might stop doing some or all of theses steps. Don't be alarmed or disheartened if that happens; it's normal. Simply jump back on the horse when you realize the change and start again, step by step.

Although this is the end of the 11 steps and the Untapped Brilliance book, your journey is just starting. These steps give you a strong foundation so that your brilliance can shine bright. I can't wait to see what you achieve.

Be sure to keep in touch and tell me how you are doing!

If you'd like extra support and coaching from me and to be part of a supportive community of kind, motivated adults living with ADHD, we'd love to welcome you into The Untapped Brilliance Club. Go to **www.untappedbrilliance.com/club** to learn more.

APPENDIX A

Your ADHD Emergency Tool Box

There are times when life is taking its toll on you despite all your best efforts. When this happens, it's time to pull out one of the tricks from your emergency tool box.

Exercise
There will be times when you are bogged down with a work project, or you feel anxious and just can't focus. You can change your mood and concentration level by doing some exercise, either your regular workout, a 10-minute speed walk, or running up and down stairs. When you return, your brain will feel more alert and you'll be able to concentrate on the task at hand more clearly.

Meditation
Once you have developed your technique and feel at ease meditating, you might try practicing it when you are feeling very tense or anxious. Just take five minutes, find a quiet corner, close your eyes and carry out your meditation technique. You'll be surprised at how calm and focused you can become in this short time!

Declutter a Small Area

If you are feeling low or depressed, try tidying up a small area that has been bugging you for a while. It doesn't matter if it's your desk or your sock drawer. There is magic in the combination of movement and seeing the organized results of your decluttering efforts. It will really boost your mood and recharge you!

Have a Healthy Snack

If you are feeling cranky, scattered and emotional, check in with yourself and ask, "When did I last eat?" It might be time for a healthy snack to re-charge those neurons!

APPENDIX B

ADHD Primer

I made the assumption that if you are reading this book then you know all about ADHD. However if you or someone you know need a quick refresher on the basics, the following primer will be useful.

What Is ADHD?

ADHD is a neurological condition that results in distractedness, impulsiveness, restlessness, disorganization and mood swings. While many people may experience these traits to some extent, people with ADHD experience them to a degree that interferes with daily living. ADHD can affect a person physically (inattention, hyperactivity, impulsivity), emotionally (mood and self-esteem issues), and socially (trouble maintaining personal relationships, jobs, etc.).

What Does ADHD Stand For?

ADHD stands for attention deficit hyperactivity disorder. If you receive an official ADHD diagnosis, you will also be told which presentation of ADHD you have. There are three presentations: predominately inattentive presentation, predominately hyperactive-impulsive presentation, or combined presentation.

A person with predominately inattentive ADHD experiences problems regulating their attention. It's hard to focus, but you can be physically still. For a detailed list of common inattentive ADHD characteristics in adults visit this article:
www.untappedbrilliance.com/adhd-inattentive

A person with predominantly hyperactive-impulsive ADHD is characterized by impulsive and hyperactive behavior. Many adults don't resonate with the term 'hyperactive' as it conjures up images of an energetic little boy. However, both men and women can have hyperactive-impulsive presentation. It's helpful to know that hyperactivity looks different in adults than in children. For example, it becomes more internal in adulthood and less obvious to a casual observer. For a detailed list of common hyperactive-impulsive ADHD characteristics in adults visit this article:
www.untappedbrilliance.com/adhd-hyperactive

The most common type of ADHD and the most researched is combined presentation. This means you have met the criteria for both inattentive and hyperactive-impulsive forms of ADHD.

There isn't a better or worse presentation to have. Remember, knowledge is power, so you are now in an excellent position to start treating and managing it in the best way for you.

Why Is ADHD Becoming More Widespread?

As we learn more about ADHD, more people are being diagnosed.

Unfortunately, there is still a lot of skepticism about ADHD and some see it as a modern illness. However, historical evidence of what we now refer to as ADHD was first mentioned in 493 BC by Hippocrates. This Greek physician and scientist described a condition featuring "...quickened responses to sensory experience, but also less tenaciousness because the soul moves on quickly to the next impression."

As we can see, his prescription for this condition has stood the test of time: "Barley rather than wheat bread, fish rather than meat, water drinks and many natural and diverse physical activities."

Typical Signs and Symptoms of ADHD

Inability to concentrate
This can have serious implications at work and study. Adults with ADHD can miss important information if they lose track of a conversation, and they may avoid activities that require a deep level of concentration. Staying on target with boring tasks is a chore. Distractedness can also cause tension in relationships if it is misinterpreted as a lack of interest.

Lack of organization
Due to problems with task planning, personal organization and time management, ADHD adults are often labeled unfavorably. Chronically late, hurried, and ill-prepared, they tend to over-commit and leave tasks unfinished. They also have difficulty setting and maintaining routines. Overwhelmed by the constant struggle just to keep their heads above water, ADHD adults are often worn down by high levels of stress.

Poor memory and forgetfulness
Adults with ADHD are more apt to lose or misplace important possessions such as passports, wallets, car keys, purses, laptops, and cell phones. They may also arrive late for meetings, appointments and lectures, or forget them altogether.

Trouble thinking clearly
Adults with ADHD find it hard to perform to their intellectual capacity. They have difficulty with intense learning situations such as lectures and in-depth reading assignments, and are prone to errors in spelling and math. Because of their tendency to become side-

tracked, key information can be missed, resulting in mistakes.

Depression and low self-esteem
Because the world is not designed to accommodate their differences, life can be a real challenge for ADHD adults. They tend to perform inconsistently (brilliant one day and dreadful the next), struggle with things that seem effortless to others and fall behind in their work. They have to deal constantly with negative feedback from people and the realization that they are not living up to their potential. This can lead to anxiety, depression and low self-esteem.

ADHD and the Executive Functions of the Brain

Research has found that numerous ADHD symptoms are caused by executive function impairment. Executive functioning is the brain's ability to initiate and control mental processes.

We can think of executive functioning as the brains project manager. The project manager's job is to instruct and coordinate the project team and ensure that each member carries out his assigned role to accomplish the objective, using the resources at his disposal. Likewise, executive function directs a "team" of central control processes in the brain that are responsible for other brain functions. The components of executive function that affect our daily life are:
- Working memory and recall
- Keeping facts in mind, manipulating information and retrieving stored data from long-term memory
- Activation, arousal, and effort
- Starting, giving attention to, and finishing a task
- Emotional control
- Enduring frustration, thinking prior to speaking or taking action
- Language internalization
- Controlling self-talk to manage actions and behavior.

- Complex problem-solving
- Breaking down a problem, examining its components and synthesizing ideas towards a solution.

What Causes ADHD?

There has been much research into this question. While the exact cause is still unknown, differences in the brains of people with ADHD compared to those without it have been found in four areas:

Anatomical differences

Research in this area has compared the size and shape of ADHD and non-ADHD brains. Differences have been found in the size and function of the corpus callosum, which connects the left and right cerebral hemispheres and mediates communication between the two.

Irregularities found in the basal ganglia may also be suggestive of ADHD. The basal ganglia are a group of structures associated with motor control, cognition and learning.

Chemical differences

The brain is made up of networks of brain cells, or neurons. Chemicals called neurotransmitters transmit messages between neurons. There are thought to be over 30 different neurotransmitters, including dopamine, norepinephrine, epinephrine, acetylcholine and serotonin, which are all related to ADHD. ADHD is associated with impaired functioning of certain neurotransmitters, particularly dopamine and norepinephrine, which is why some stimulant medications are effective at treating symptoms such as impulsivity, hyperactivity and impaired cognitive performance.

Functional differences

Certain differences in brain functioning have been noted in people with ADHD.

Frontal lobe
Researchers have found that, during concentration, frontal lobe activity decreases in ADHD subjects, but increases in control subjects. The frontal lobe is vital to many of the brain's executive functions.

Limbic system
The limbic system is found in the center of the brain and is associated with feelings and emotions. Increased limbic activity as well as decreased frontal lobe activity has been found in people with ADHD compared to controls.

Parietal lobe
The parietal lobe is positioned behind the frontal lobe. ADHD has been associated with increased activity in this region.

Genetics

There is a strong genetic component to ADHD. It is more likely that a child will be born with ADHD if one of the biological parents has ADHD. This percentage increases if both parents have ADHD.

However, even if a child inherits genetic characteristics related to ADHD, it does not mean they will have ADHD. While genes do play a part in ADHD, so does the environment, and it is a combination of the two that will determine if the ADHD will be activated. While the exact genetic factors are not exactly known, it is thought that the genes DAT1 and DRD4 could be responsible for heritable ADHD.

Adults Have ADHD Too!

Most people are aware that children can have ADHD, but they don't realize adults can have it, too. While one-third of children who have ADHD outgrow it, the rest carry their ADHD into adulthood.

Many adults have already developed techniques subconsciously to compensate for their ADHD. Take a look at your own life and give yourself credit for all the creative ways you have managed with ADHD so far!

APPENDIX C

Charts

Over the next few pages are charts to help you with the exercises in the book. You can also download full-page versions of these charts from **www.UntappedBrilliance.com/chartsfromthebook**

Success Journal

Write down compliments, actions you are proud of and anything else that makes you feel good. Writing them down here will help you remember them and cheer you up, inspire you and propel you forward.

DATE	COMPLIMENT OR FEEL-GOOD ACTION

JACQUELINE SINFIELD

My Exercise Chart

Month of _____

DATE	TYPE OF EXERCISE	CHECK MARK OR STAR	NOTES
1			
2			
3			
4			
5			
6			
7			
8			
9			
10			
11			
12			
13			
14			
15			

16			
17			
18			
19			
20			
21			
22			
23			
24			
25			
26			
27			
28			
29			
30			
31			

Don't wait to the beginning of the month or week. Start your exercise today!

JACQUELINE SINFIELD

My Meditation Chart

Month of _____

DATE	MEDITATION	CHECK MARK OR STAR	NOTES
1			
2			
3			
4			
5			
6			
7			
8			
9			
10			
11			
12			
13			
14			
15			

16			
17			
18			
19			
20			
21			
22			
23			
24			
25			
26			
27			
28			
29			
30			
31			

Don't wait to the beginning of the month or week.
Start your meditation today!

Decluttering List

Every home is different in terms of size and the number and type of storage space. This is a guide to help you declutter. Use it as a prompt and guide to ensure that all areas of your home are addressed. Feel free to adapt the list to suit your home.

KITCHEN	KITCHEN
Under the Kitchen sink * * * *	Refrigerator and Freezer * * * *
Kitchen cupboards 1 * * * 2 * * * 3 * * * 4 * * * 5 * * *	Kitchen Drawers 1 * * * 2 * * * 3 * * * 4 * * * 5 * * *

Kitchen Counter Top * * *	Kitchen Table * * *
BATHROOM Under the Bathroom Sink * * *	**BATHROOM** Medicine Cabinet * * *
Bathroom counter top * *	Bath (if you use this as a storage space) * *
FAMILY OR LIVING ROOM Windowsills * * * *	**FAMILY OR LIVING ROOM** Other flat surface * * * *
DVD and CD storage * * *	Book Cases * * *
Magazine rack * * * *	Coffee Table * * * *

BEDROOM 1	BEDROOM 2
1st Bedside table * * * 2nd Bedside table * * *	1st Bedside table * * * 2nd Bedside table * * *
Bookshelf * * * *	Bookshelf * * * *

BEDROOM 1 CONTINUED	BEDROOM 2 CONTINUED
Under the bed * * * *	Under the bed * * * *
Wardrobe * * * *	Wardrobe * * * *
Chest of Drawers Draw 1 Draw 2 Draw 3	Chest of Drawers Draw 1 Draw 2 Draw 3

ENTRANCE HALL	ENTRANCE HALL
Coat Storage * * *	Shoe Storage * * *
Key storage area *	
HOME OFFICE	**HOME OFFICE**
Desk * * *	Filing cabinet * * *

Big Picture Chart

Follow the directions outlined in Step Seven and write down everything that comes to mind. Remember, think BIG! Don't censor yourself; whatever springs to mind, write it down.

8-week Plan

From _____ to _____

GOAL	ACTIONS	DO-ABLE ACTIONS	ADDN'L INFO
Exercise daily to help ADHD symptoms	Find out options for exercise I could do at home	--Ask Sally the name of the exercise app she uses --Google 'exercises you can do at home' --Go to bottom of my closet and get my sneakers	

2-ish Year Plan

	ITEM OR DESIRE	APPROXIMATE TIME OF STARTING	CHECK WHEN COMPLETED!
1			
2			
3			
4			
5			
6			
7			
8			
9			
10			
11			
12			
13			
14			
15			
16			
17			
18			

Anti-procrastination List

Run around your home and write down all those odd jobs you have been meaning to do but keep putting off. Once they are on this list you will be able to start working through them and the sense of relief will be huge. Aim for list of 101 items.

	ITEM TO DO	ESTIMATED TIME TO COMPLETE TASK	USEFUL INFO RELATED TO ITEM	CHECK WHEN COMPLETED
1				
2				
3				
4				
5				
6				
7				
8				
9				
10				
11				
12				
13				
14				
15				
16				
17				
18				

JACQUELINE SINFIELD

19				
20				
21				
22				
23				
24				
25				
26				
27				
28				
29				
30				
31				
32				
33				
34				
35				
36				
37				
38				
39				
40				
41				
42				
43				
44				
45				

UNTAPPED BRILLIANCE

46				
47				
48				
49				
50				
51				
52				
53				
54				
55				
56				
57				
58				
59				
60				
61				
62				
63				
64				
65				
66				
67				
68				
69				
70				
71				
72				
73				

74				
75				
76				
77				
78				
79				
80				
81				
82				
83				
84				
85				
86				
87				
88				
89				
90				
91				
92				
93				
94				
95				
96				
97				
98				
99				
100				
101				

Daily To Do List

Today will be a GREAT day if I accomplish…..

	ITEM	CHECK WHEN COMPLETED
1		
2		
3		

Today will be a GREAT day if I accomplish…..

	ITEM	CHECK WHEN COMPLETED
1		
2		
3		

Have Fun!

What is fun for you? Use these exercises to find out and make plans to have more of it!

NAME AS MANY OF THE THINGS YOU DID LAST WEEK AS YOU CAN REMEMBER	WAS IT FUN OR NOT FUN?	IF IT WAS FUN, WHEN/HOW CAN YOU DO MORE OF IT?

Become a Weekend Warrior

SATURDAY Time of Day	ACTIVITY	WITH WHO?

SUNDAY Time of Day	ACTIVITY	WITH WHO?

Make Themes!

RITUAL or ACTIVITY	POTENTIAL THEMES	CHOSEN THEME

APPENDIX D

Recommended Resources

www.untappedbrilliance.com

Step 1

Books
Driven to Distraction
Delivered from Distraction
both by Edward M Hallowell and John J Ratey

Website
www.drsears.com

Step 2

Books
Perricone Diet by Nicholas Perricone
The Zone by Dr. Barry Sears

Apps & Websites
Noom
www.realage.com

Step 4

Meditation Apps
Insight Timer
The Tapping Solution
Calm

Step 6

Books
Sink Reflections by Marla Cilley, the Flylady
Speed Cleaning by Jeff Campbell

Website
www.flylady.net

Step 8

Book
Feel the Fear and Do It Anyway by Susan Jeffers

Step 9

Website
www.toastmasters.org

Step 10

Books
How to Win Friends and Influence People by Dale Carnegie

Websites
www.linkedin.com
www.facebook.com
www.meetup.com
www.untappedbrilliance.com/club

Step 11

Books
The Best Year of Your Life by Debbie Ford

About the Author

Jacqueline Sinfield has been an ADHD coach since 2005. She has helped thousands of adults learn ADHD-friendly strategies, including organization, time management, and kindness towards themselves so they can reach their full potential in all areas of their lives.

Before becoming a coach, Jacqueline trained and worked as a nurse in England. She established her international coaching practice when she moved to Montreal, Canada.

Jacqueline now runs The Untapped Brilliance Club, an ADHD group coaching membership.

Her Untapped Brilliance blog has won multiple "Best ADHD Blog" awards.

To learn many more ways to manage your ADHD brain successfully, visit Jacqueline's blog at **www.untappedbrilliance.com**

The Untapped Brilliance Club

If you loved this book and want personalized help, then **The Untapped Brilliance Club** would be a great next step for you!

The Untapped Brilliance Club is the perfect combination of knowledge, encouragement, action, and community.

This membership program is designed to help you learn ADHD friendly strategies and implement them into your life so you feel organized, productive, and great about yourself!

The Untapped Brilliance Club Membership includes:

- Live group coaching calls with me, Jacqueline, to get your own ADHD-related questions personally answered.
- My **entire** library of ADHD-friendly courses.
- Eight-week planning workshops every other month, so you can plan and follow through successfully on your goals.
- Theme of the Month with new, fun, super-practical lessons and strategies, so you never get bored in the group.
- Real-time accountability, so it's easier for you to take action
- An incredibly supportive community of positive, proactive adults also living with ADHD.

Head to www.untappedbrilliance.com/club, while it's fresh in your mind, for all the details!

Made in the USA
Columbia, SC
21 February 2023